DAVID & BETH GRANT

BEYOND THE SHAME

Project Rescue's Fight to Restore Dignity to Survivors of Sexual Slavery

Foreword by
DARY AND BONNIE NORTHROP

Beyond the Shame

Project Rescue's Fight to Restore Dignity to Survivors of Sexual Slavery

By David and Beth Grant

Printed in the United States of America

Second Printing

ISBN: 1-880689-33-2

Copyright 2013, David and Beth Grant and Onward Books, Inc.

Cover and interior design by Keith Locke, CauseCreates.com

Unless otherwise indicated, all Scripture references are from the
Holy Bible: New International Version, copyright 1984,
Zondervan Bible Publishers.

DEDICATION

Dedicated to our colleagues who have affiliated with Project Rescue and courageously pioneered ministries to women and children in sexual slavery—and children at risk—over the past 16 years. Through their relentless, Spirit-empowered efforts in places of formidable darkness, survivors of exploitation are discovering freedom, healing, and hope as children of God:

K.K. Devaraj, India
Doug & Ramona Jacobs, Nepal
Ambika Pandey, India
Mathew & Suha Daniel, India
Beth Decker, India
Easo & Leela Daniel, India
Sumi Samuel, India
Arul Santosh, India
Nancy & Andy Raatz, Moldova
Vinita & Rohit Bhalla, India

Rebecca Grant Shults, India
Lucy & Kevin Donaldson, India
Rajnish and Orina Jacobs, India
Lisa Russi, Bangladesh
Mel and Jillian Rogers, Bangladesh
Ruth Baroi, Bangladesh
Eve Austin &
Umeda, Central Eurasia
Fiona Bellshaw &
Juan Carlos Escobar, Spain

We also express special appreciation to Rescue: Freedom International President Jeremy Vallerand and Chairman Dick Foth for enthusiastically sharing our passion to empower the Project Rescue team to provide life-changing care for the victims of the injustice of trafficking.

AUTHORS' NOTE

Sexual slavery is a $32-billion "industry" that extends to every continent. The profiteers remain a threat to their victims and to the workers endeavoring to rescue them. Thus, the names of the women and children portrayed in Beyond the Shame *have been changed and their locations concealed. In addition, for their protection and to enhance reader interest, dialog has been created and some details have been altered.*

C O N T E N T S

ENDORSEMENTS

David and Beth Grant's passion to rescue women and children trapped in the web of human trafficking and provide them with an opportunity for a new life is inspiring. Through their dedication and hard work, the ministry of Project Rescue has raised the standard of best practices in the field. My life and ministry were deeply impacted when David and Beth took me to a Saturday night church service in the heart of Mumbai's red-light district. There I saw firsthand what the grace of God can do in the lives of those who have been victimized by the lust and greed of others. There is room at the Cross for you.

Omar Beiler
Eurasia Regional Director
Assemblies of God World Missions

As a survivor of sexual assault, I'm so grateful for the healing words provided for those suffering the aftermath of shame and guilt. May those who read these words find hope, joy, peace, but most importantly, freedom! May the documented stories remind us to put a name and a face to the millions still in slavery.

Christine Caine
Best-selling Author and Founder
The A21 Campaign

Reading *Beyond the Shame* brings conflicting powerful emotions—anger at evil, pain in sharing the suffering, and rejoicing in the redemption. The next question is "What can I do?" Here you will find your answer! David and Beth Grant are not newcomers to this field. They were in the trenches before most people even knew the term "human trafficking." This is a long awaited book for these times!

Jo Anne Lyon
General Superintendent
The Wesleyan Church

Project Rescue is an exemplary ministry of compassion. Its commitment to fight against one of the most aberrant and cruel tragedies of our times is unquestionable. My wife, Fiona, and I have been deeply impacted by the work of Beth and David Grant, who in such a clear and humble way have sensitized and brought awareness to many to this present reality in the majority of the world. Although India may be an evident setting of sexual slavery, human trafficking has invaded the West like an insatiable devourer. The Church, together with Project Rescue, must extend hands of compassion to those trapped in modern day slavery and rescue them from this perverse power of darkness.

Juan Carlos Escobar
General Superintendent
Spain Assemblies of God

8

As a leader in the Assemblies of God, I have watched the early days
and now years of development of the compassionate ministry of
Project Rescue to sexually exploited women and children in India
and beyond. Under the leadership of David and Beth Grant, Project
Rescue has become respected among those working with trafficking
victims around the world both in and outside the faith community.
Now, *Beyond the Shame* provides those of us who have prayed and
partnered with them an opportunity to share in the celebration
of hard-won healing and freedom. It is not an easy story, but it
is compelling. When good people engage their faith on behalf of
victims of injustice, there is a new life of God-given dignity beyond
the shame of sexual slavery and prostitution through Christ.

Dr. George O. Wood
General Superintendent
U.S. Assemblies of God

While there is a heightened awareness concerning the problem of
child trafficking and sexual slavery in our world today, this increased
interest and desire for involvement is not always accompanied by an
adequate understanding of ground realities. In *Beyond the Shame*
David and Beth Grant bring a lifetime of majority world experience
and many years of actual personal engagement in their treatment
of this burning issue. Carefully documented firsthand testimony
is skillfully woven into an authentic and riveting insider's account,
as David and Beth lend a credible voice to the victims of the most
loathsome social evil of our times. This book is a must read because of
its wealth of information and insight, but even more so because of the
deep sensitivity and passion with which the authors present their case,
in a stirring challenge to the social conscience of the church and the
world community.

Ivan Satyavrata
Pastor
Kolkata, India

ACKNOWLEDGMENTS

From the very first phone call from K.K. Devaraj—asking if we could start a safe home for 37 girls from the red-light district in Bombay—until today, we have known this mission was God's. We have been blessed to serve Him and see thousands of lives touched by His love and healing power.

But God uses people to accomplish His purposes, and Project Rescue wouldn't exist without the blessing of our Assemblies of God World Missions leadership and our dedicated support team. Our deep appreciation goes to our Executive Director Greg Mundis, Regional Director Omar Beiler and Area Director Bob McGurty, who have been supportive as we dared to dream what God might do in the darkest of places if we took Jesus there.

Special thanks to the members of our support team who are gifts from God to Project Rescue ministries and to us personally. Because they are called and faithful to their respective responsibilities, we have been released to fulfill the tasks to which God has called us. They are living 1 Corinthians 3:8-9: "The one who plants and the one who waters have one purpose, and they will each be rewarded according to their own labor. For we are co-workers in God's service."

HUMAN TRAFFICKING FACTS

The following statistics are the most conservative estimates available.

- 27 million people worldwide are victims of modern day slavery.[1]
- 2 million children are exploited by the international commercial sex trade.[2]
- $32 billion in profits (in U.S. dollars) are generated annually by the human trafficking industry.[3]
- 80 percent of those sold into sexual slavery are under 24, and some are as young as six.[4]
- 90 percent of the women and girls between the ages of 15-35 in Bangladesh brothels take steroids to make themselves more attractive to clients, but the side effects are devastating.[5]
- 250,000 Nepalese girls are believed to be working in the sex industry in India, according to the Coalition Against Trafficking in Women (CATW).[6]
- 40 percent of the prostituted women in India enter into sexual slavery before age 18.[7]
- 40,000 children in Moldova have been left without either parent due to the migration of adults in search of work—leaving the children at greater risk of trafficking, forced labor and sexual exploitation.[8]
- 90 percent of prostituted women in Spain are controlled by organized crime networks.[9]

FOREWORD

When the initial shock that slavery could exist today finally wore off, we both knew we had to do something about it. But we were deterred by the enormity of the problem and the mind-numbing statistics. All that changed, however, when we saw the work of Project Rescue firsthand.

We witnessed the chaos of the red-light districts of Mumbai and Kolkata. We saw the hollow, despairing eyes of the prostituted women and girls in the streets. We understood why human trafficking and sexual slavery have been called the darkest, most hellish things on earth. The brothels are filthy, smelly, ugly and filled with the tragic stories of women and children who endure abuse day after day.

Conversely, we felt the peaceful presence of God in the Project Rescue aftercare homes and saw the joy radiating from the faces of rescued women and girls. Their lives have been transformed. Once living in dungeon-like brothels, they now have the hope of Jesus Christ.

The global task of ending human trafficking and sexual slavery is daunting, but God has given each person the ability to make a significant difference in this fight for freedom. Together, we can stem the tide of human trafficking. Lives can be rescued and changed forever. It happens every day at Project Rescue aftercare homes. The homes are indeed a place ripe with God's promises and plans. Each day, mothers and children sing in heartfelt worship to Jesus. They are grateful for His love and mercy and thankful to those who have given them a home where they feel loved and valued.

On our visit to the homes, little girls with wide smiles grabbed our hands to proudly show us their bunk beds and cupboards. Rather than hiding under their mother's bed in the brothel, they now have a place they call their own. Each morning they awaken to a warm meal and dress themselves in clean clothes. Their childhood has indeed been recaptured.

The women in Project Rescue's vocational centers also radiated with pride, as we admired their beautiful handcrafted items. Formerly valued as a commodity to purchase, now, these women have the opportunity to learn a vocational skill, acquire a sustainable income, and pursue an education. They are discovering their true value as God's daughters and celebrating their precious individuality and unique abilities.

Our initial visit to Project Rescue in India changed our lives. When we returned to Colorado, we launched the U COUNT Campaign—an anti-trafficking ministry. Currently, a team of dedicated men and women work diligently to support both local and global anti-trafficking endeavors, with our primary focus to help provide economic escape and safe living and working environments through our partnership with Project Rescue sites in India and Nepal.

Our overwhelming gratitude and respect goes to David and Beth Grant for recognizing a horrific need and courageously taking action to change it. Eternity is different because of this ministry and the laborers who have joined them in this fight for freedom.

Beyond the Shame is a painfully honest portrait of human trafficking and sexual slavery. The pages of this book will take you into that world. And, hopefully, as a result, you will join us by doing your part to put an end to one of the world's greatest injustices.

— Dary and Bonnie Northrop
Lead Pastors, Timberline Church
Fort Collins, Colorado

INTRODUCTION

Ten-year-old Nina awakens to the bustling sounds of Falkland Road, in the heart of Mumbai, India: honking, clanging and shouting.

She readies herself for the first of many men and the horrors of another day. Her life—and her body—are not her own.

Tragically Nina is one of 21 million women and children[1] who are trapped in a $32-billion (annually) sex "industry."[2] But this is not a new phenomenon. Prostitution in some form has existed in every culture, in every city as far back as the Book of Genesis.

Amy Carmichael, better known as Amma (which means "mother"), was a pioneer in outreach to prostituted women and girls. She went to India in 1890 to rescue girls sold as prostitutes to the Hindu temples, where men came to have sex as a form of worship to their gods.

Today, however, sexual slavery is fueled by economics. Millions of women are trafficked for profit from countries in Asia, Africa, Latin America and Europe. More than 1 million minors are victims, with the average age being 14.[3] In the United States alone, an estimated 100,000 children are exploited each year.[4] Johns Hopkins University defines sex trafficking as "the recruitment, transportation (within national or across international borders), transfer, harboring, or receipt of persons for the purposes of commercial sexual exploitation. Sex trafficking is accomplished by means of fraud, deception, threat of, or use of force, abuse of a position of vulnerability, and other forms of coercion."[5]

PREYING ON THE POOR

Global sex trafficking tends to flow from the poorer nations—where poverty creates desperation—to the richer nations.

Economic profitability has attracted organized crime to the business of sex trafficking. A girl purchased for $200, for example, can generate $10,000 a month.[6] The World Wide Web has only served to increase profit margins and expand the epidemic by providing an inexpensive and far-reaching marketing tool for prostitution and trafficking.

Lisa Thompson, a noted expert on the injustice of human trafficking, says, "In particular, economic factors like poverty, lack of education, lack of job opportunities, gender factors, and lack of proper registration/citizenship papers act as powerful forces, pushing women and children in vulnerability for sex trafficking."[7]

Phyliss Kilbourn, a global advocate for the victims of sex trafficking, says, "One shudders to think of the sheer terror, pain, indignity, and shame inflicted on women and children forced to become a commodity of the massive global, multimillion-dollar sex industry. Their degrading experiences are incomprehensible, resulting in a warped sense of their true identity. Tragically, the measuring rod of their personal value radically shifts from being rooted in the truth of being created in the image of God with inherent worth to being defined by such factors as age and virginity, the amount of profit they can generate for perpetrators of evil, or how they can be used as markets of exploitation. In the aftermath of a trafficking experience, the physical and psychological control tactics used by traffickers, combined with the physical and sexual abuses perpetrated, leave both deep emotional scars and physical damage. Sexual abuse also results in significant spiritual losses. Therefore, complete restoration for those who have been sexually trafficked must be holistic."[8]

Worldwide, prostituted women have a shorter life expectancy due to violence, suicide, AIDS and more. For many, the wounds of abuse are visible: burn marks on their arms from being tortured following a failed escape; or scars on their wrists from an attempted suicide. For others, the wounds are hidden, but just as real and deadly. Emotional abuse, mental illness and disease have taken their toll. In Mumbai, India, for example, more than 80 percent of the women and children rescued out of the brothels are HIV positive ... and, yet, most are unaware they have the disease.

ASSETS AND LIABILITIES

In many majority-world countries, boys are considered a "blessing" or an asset to the family. Girls, on the other hand, are viewed as a liability. Thus, there is seldom remorse when a father sells his daughter into slavery or opts to have a female child aborted.

Because every human life is created by God and stamped with His image (Genesis 1:27), God's children have a biblical responsibility to pronounce value on women and children. Woman was created as an equal partner and helper for man, to serve alongside him as a steward of the Earth (Genesis 2:18). Together they were given authority over the life forms God created (Genesis 1:28-30). But today, the God-given value of women and children is under attack. And, for that reason, Project Rescue was established: to fight for freedom and justice for women and children who have been devalued and victimized by sexual slavery. Isaiah 61:1-3 serves as a mandate for Project Rescue and other defenders of justice: "Bind up the brokenhearted, to proclaim freedom for the captives and release ... for the prisoners ... to comfort all who mourn, and provide for those who grieve ... to bestow on them a crown of beauty instead of ashes, the oil of joy instead of mourning, and a garment of praise instead of a spirit of despair."

Many churches, civic groups, corporations and elected officials have joined with Project Rescue in a bold and courageous form of compassion. Global Christian Life Church, in Delhi, India, where Robert Jeyaraj is pastor, is an example of a congregation that incorporated rescuing women and children from the red-light district into the church's mission. Today GCLC members are catalysts for other congregations to reach out to prostituted women and children in their communities. (See Appendix III for guidelines on how local churches can effectively fight sex trafficking in their communities.)

Isaiah 59:15-16 says, "The Lord looked and was

displeased that there was no justice. He ... was appalled that there was no one to intervene." Not every person is called, or equipped, to "intervene" in places like Mumbai, India, or Madrid, Spain. But everyone can play a part in rescuing women and children from the clutches of prostitution and abuse. College students, for example, have joined with Project Rescue to hold art auctions; mothers have run marathons; business leaders have designated a portion of their profits; and children have held fundraisers at school and in their neighborhoods to make a stand for justice. (See Appendix III for practical ways to fight for the freedom of prostituted women and children.)

THE BEGINNING

Years ago, we were not engaged in the fight to liberate trafficked women and children and to nurture them back to health. But that changed in 1997 when we received a call from K.K. Devaraj, director of Bombay Teen Challenge in Mumbai, India. He had just conducted a church service on Falkland Road, and more than 100 prostituted women had indicated their desire to follow Jesus. They soon discovered 100,000 women and girls were serving as sex slaves in the infamous Kamatapura red-light district at that time. Many of the prostituted women begged Devaraj to take their daughters, so they could escape the horrors of brothel life. Devaraj phoned us to ask if, together, we could open a home for 37 children. Without knowing the cost involved or where this journey would take us, we agreed. That was the beginning of Project Rescue.

Weeks later, we visited the red-light district to learn more about the plight of the women and children living there. It was after midnight and thousands of men were converging on the brothels. It was both horrifying and heartbreaking. David looked up at the dark sky and said, "God, there are over one million prostituted girls in India. How can I only ask You to help us reach out to a few thousand? Will You help us rescue one million from these streets and bring them into Your family?"

We opened our first aftercare home in Mumbai with 37 children. Within six months, more than 100 children were engaged, as word spread about a safe haven where the physical, medical, social, educational and spiritual needs of children were being met. Children who had spent days shuddering under the beds of their abused mothers, now had a safe bed to call their own.

LONG-TERM COMMITMENT

One afternoon a madam from the red-light district phoned Devaraj. One of the women in her brothel had broken down emotionally and was running through the streets of the red-light district completely naked.

"Do you want her?" she asked coldly.

Before Devaraj could respond, she added, "She's worthless to me."

Devaraj nodded. "Yes, we want her."

Devaraj and outreach team members eventually located the tormented woman and took her into their care. For eighteen months, the team provided physical, emotional, and spiritual assistance and saw the woman return to health. She grew in her understanding of God's love, too, and eventually graduated from the program as a trophy of His grace.

The madam's initial question to Devaraj is a critical one for each person to consider: "Do you want her?" she asked. Devaraj knew if he replied "yes," he was making a long-term commitment to nurture the woman back to physical, emotional and spiritual health. If we, too, are serious about restoring victims of sexual slavery to wholeness, we must be willing to engage in a healing process that often takes years to accomplish. In other words, when we declare God's value on a human life and extend a helping hand, we must realize that "rescuing" a person from sexual slavery is more than a one-time event. It is a process that requires a long-term commitment.

God desires that every woman and child victimized by sexual slavery experience abundant life. But, for that to happen, we must go beyond rescuing them from prostitution or participating in awareness campaigns. It demands aftercare, rehabilitation and restoration. Unless there is emotional and spiritual support waiting for them, many women will return to the brothels within a matter of weeks of their escape.

Today there are 15 Project Rescue affiliated ministry sites in six countries, where women and children are on a journey to wholeness. Because of the complexity of the issue, collaboration is essential. Pastors, trauma counselors, medical leaders, and social workers all play a significant role in each phase of healing. Taking the time to build relationships with the women and children is critical, because healing does not happen without trust.

Project Rescue believes three truths guide the healing process:

1. No true rescue can take place without the love and transformational power of Jesus Christ.

2. For compassionate ministry to be life changing, the presentation of God's Word and deeds must go hand in hand.

3. No social action is value free. Our compassion grows out of our relationship with Jesus Christ, and acts of compassion are a natural extension of His work in our lives.

Because of the efforts of churches and organizations like Project Rescue, many women have experienced lasting hope. They have embraced Isaiah 54:4: "Do not be afraid; you will not be put to shame. Do not fear disgrace; you will not be humiliated. You will forget the shame of your youth." They have moved "beyond the shame" and experienced healing and purpose. It is difficult to believe that some once stood on street corners, dressed provocatively, essentially inviting men to have sex with them. Their eyes were once dead, their smiles like stone. But today, joy has supplanted sorrow. They have a future; they have meaningful relationships; and they have a friend in Jesus.

Their transformation is celebrated when the women

walk across the platform to receive their graduation certificate from one of our schools or discipleship programs. For most, when their names are announced and the room erupts in applause, it is the first time in their entire lives that they have been recognized for an accomplishment. Adorned in colorful dresses or saris, they accept their diplomas as tears of gratitude often stream down their faces. For them, it is a moment to reflect on the life they once led and to lay claim to God's promise that He will "never leave or forsake" them.

During each graduation ceremony, we marvel at the transformation of beautiful young women. After enduring years of sexual slavery, they have been nurtured back to health and hope for a better life restored. And, because of their newfound faith in Jesus, they need never again be bought, bartered or betrayed. Time and again, graduates share the same refrain: "I was once in bondage, but now I am free—because Jesus is for me."

Unfortunately not every woman's story ends in celebration. Some have succumbed to threats and returned to the brothels; others, after years of abuse, have died prematurely. Yet, their stories serve as a reminder that we must continue the fight to offer hope to victims of sexual slavery. That is the reason we wrote *Beyond the Shame*: that the stories of these 14 women and children would compel readers to move beyond pity to action. May many more victims experience freedom because readers were willing to ask themselves one important question: "What can I do?"

— David and Beth Grant

That night Adrienne finally

relented and fell asleep after

pounding the walls and

shouting for help until her

voice was merely a rasp.

CHAPTER 1

ADRIENNE

It was Sunday morning and light snow fell outside the drafty village church. From her rickety rough-hewn pew, 17-year-old Adrienne could hear the preaching and singing, but her mind was elsewhere. Dreams of completing school, being married, and having a home of her own monopolized her thoughts. But, first, she told herself, she needed to find a way to earn some money. Her cousin had located a job for her in the city, many miles away, but Adrienne hadn't mustered the courage to ask her father's permission.

I must ask him today, Adrienne told herself, *or I will lose my chance at the job.*

As she and her father strode home, the snow crunching under their feet, Adrienne cleared her throat. "Papa," she stammered. "When I'm done with my studies, can I take a job in the city? Cousin Eugene has found me a good-paying job."

Abruptly the crunching under his feet stopped.

"When did you learn of this?" he asked in an

agitated tone.

"He sent me a letter last week, saying it's a very good job in a factory."

"It's not safe," he replied in a stately, baritone voice.

"I'm not a child anymore," she whined. "Think of all the money I can earn that will help our family. Please let me go."

Papa lowered his head as if weighing his decision. "I don't know. How would you get there?"

"Eugene promised to buy me a bus ticket if I came."

"How long would you stay?"

"Just a year," Adrienne pledged. "By then I'll make enough money to come home. Trust me—I won't disappoint you."

Without a response, Papa resumed walking.

Trailing closely behind him, Adrienne couldn't decide if he was angry ... or just worried about losing his oldest daughter.

Later that evening, a tap came to the door of the room shared by Adrienne and her two younger sisters.

"Adrienne," Papa said.

"Yes, Papa," Adrienne replied.

With a chin like steel and his voice firm, Papa said, "I have made my decision."

He paused and peered into her eyes. Anticipating his

next words, Adrienne's heart skipped a beat.

"You may go to the city, but no longer than a year," he declared.

Adrienne threw her arms around him, saying, "Thank you, Papa—you won't be sorry."

Papa wanted to launch into a lecture on the dangers of life in the city, but instead he held his little girl tight and fought to hold back his tears.

CITY LIFE

As the bus barreled into the city, Adrienne felt like a kid entering a new and different world: large buildings, a maze of automobiles, stores stacked with merchandise, and mobs of pedestrians.

When the bus finally reached its destination, a wide-eyed Adrienne hopped off like a schoolgirl in search of a parent. But Eugene was nowhere to be found.

"Eugene," her voice bellowed in the crowded bus station. "Eugene ... Eugene."

Just as panic was about to rear its ugly head, Adrienne heard a voice at her back.

"Hi, I'm Michael, a friend of Eugene's."

Adrienne turned to see a clean-shaven man in his twenties.

"Eugene had to work," he said. "He asked me to pick

you up."

Michael grabbed her suitcase, loaded it into the taxi, and opened the door for her to climb in. Adrienne hesitated, unnerved by Eugene's absence and the bloodshot eyes and spiked hair of the taxi driver.

"Everything's good," Michael said. "Please, we must hurry to meet Eugene."

Fifteen minutes later, the taxi arrived at a dull apartment complex. Michael paid the taxi driver and led Adrienne up a cold, dark staircase to the third floor.

"Been to the city before?" he asked.

"No—my first time."

"I think you'll like it here."

Entering the barren apartment, Adrienne was relieved to find a lumpy couch that was calling for her weary body.

"Is there anything you need?" Michael asked.

Adrienne shook her head. "When will Eugene be home?"

"Real soon. How about some food?" he asked.

"Right now, I just need some sleep," she replied.

"Great. Then while you're napping I'll go register your passport and legal documents with the local authorities. It won't take long."

Surrendering her papers, Adrienne stretched out on the couch and closed her eyes. She didn't even hear the door close behind Michael.

Two hours later, she awoke to an empty, stuffy apartment.

Still no Eugene or Michael.

Adrienne pulled back the curtains to open some windows—but there were none. She turned the doorknob to step outside—but the door was locked. She searched for a telephone—but there wasn't one. Instantly the apartment felt like a prison cell and fear raced through her like poison in a bloodstream.

That night Adrienne finally relented and fell asleep after pounding the walls and shouting for help until her voice was merely a rasp.

THE RETURN

The next day the knob suddenly turned and the door cracked open. Michael, accompanied by a sturdy woman with thick makeup and long black hair, reappeared.

"Where's Eugene? Why didn't you come back?" Adrienne snapped.

"You stupid girl," the woman cackled. "Come here, I want to look at you."

Adrienne froze.

"She told you to come here," Michael yelled, his words laced with profanities.

The woman measured Adrienne with her eyes

and smiled.

"You were right, Michael: She is very pretty—she will do well."

"Do well at what? What are you talking about?" Adrienne asked with a bite of fear.

"Shut up!" the woman shouted. "You don't say a word unless I ask you to."

"Where's Eugene?" Adrienne repeated.

"Do as you're told or you'll never see Eugene again!" Michael barked. "From now on you'll be working for us at a bar."

Reality struck her like a sledgehammer and she buried her tear-stained face in her hands.

"The bar is well-suited for you," the woman announced, her words hanging in the air so everyone knew she was in charge. "You will drink wine. You will dance with men and then have sex with them."

"No, I will not do what you say," Adrienne protested. "I'm a virgin—I would rather die."

"You're a virgin?" the woman cackled. "We'll make even more money."

"Get some rest—you're going to need it," Michael added coldly.

Adrienne pounded on the door long after her captors made their exit. She beat her fists against the wood until they

by sexual slavery.

Upon hearing Adrienne's story, Oxana, the Project Rescue counselor, rose from her chair and wrapped her arms around the tearful girl. "You're safe here," Oxana said. "You are not to blame for what happened to you. There is no condemnation here—only love and respect."

"But even my family blames me," she said under a waterfall of tears. "Why did God allow this to happen to me? What did I do to lose my family?"

"No one should have to endure the things you have," Oxana said. "But this is not your doing ... or God's doing. He's the One who rescued you and brought you here. And He will heal you. Someday He'll bring your family back, too."

"I can't believe in a God who would let this happen," Adrienne said. "And my family ... they say I'm dead in their eyes."

Oxana nodded. "I understand, but in time you'll see how much God loves you."

Adrienne wiped more tears from her eyes. "All I wanted was a little money, a future, and a family of my own ... and it cost me everything."

"God's concerned about your future, too," Oxana said. "He wants you to be happy. He wants to give you a family. But right now He wants you to experience His love. Because His love will heal your pain and one day restore everything you've lost."

Adrienne shook her head. "I want to believe that, but ..."

"Listen, I don't have the words to answer all your questions. There are some questions only God can answer," Oxana said. "All I know is that His love brought you through this ordeal alive ... and He will finish the work He started."

"How?" Adrienne asked skeptically.

"I don't know—but we're glad God brought you here. This is your home now ... we are your family ... and we love you."

Adrienne's tears intensified into deep sobs. Her entire body shook with pain and remorse. Once again, Oxana wrapped her arms around her new friend, saying, "Let it out, Adrienne. Just let it out. Everything is going to be all right—I promise."

Frequently the boy was too

weak to crawl out from under

the bed when his mother

entertained clients. Instead he

lay there in silence, laboring

for every breath.

CHAPTER 2

HEMA

The girls in the brothel knew him as "Sir." At 53, he was taller than most and cut an imposing figure. His ruthless tactics and dark, menacing eyes kept his sex slaves in line. They knew they had to generate profits or suffer the consequences of his wrath. Since inheriting the brothel from his father, Sir lived by two rules: Trust no one, and turn a profit. He let no one stand in his way. Rumor had it he killed two men who threatened his business; and he didn't hesitate to "mark" his girls with a knife or his fists if they didn't produce.

One night, after collecting his earnings from the girls, he debated which slave he wanted for himself. He settled on Hema. She had lived in the brothel 11 years and knew how to please him. Entering her cubicle, Sir ordered Hema's 5-year-old son, Solomon, to leave.

"Now," he shouted.

The boy stumbled outside.

Hema stood and, like she had many times before, surrendered herself to Sir. *I pray he doesn't beat me tonight,* she told herself. Lying on the bed, her eyes fell on the spine of the Bible she'd been given by her new friends at Project Rescue. She remembered Psalm 56:3 and quoted it to herself: *"When I am afraid, I put my trust in you."*

Hema kept her newfound faith in Jesus private. If Sir found out, a beating would follow. He would not tolerate anything that interfered with his business.

Without a word, Sir dropped a few coins on Hema's bed and left the room. Solomon returned as his mama placed the coins in her pouch. He fell onto the bed and looked up at his mother. She wiped the perspiration from his forehead and patted his back as a signal that she was all right.

"Jesus," she whispered, "if You are real, help me and my son leave this place. I don't want him to grow up in a brothel. If You can be raised from a grave, I believe You can give us a real home."

The brothel was the only playground Solomon knew. Sir refused to let the boy accompany his mother to the market for fear they would run away. So, Solomon and the other children of prostituted women spent their days exploring the bowels of the brothel. If not for an open area in the center of the complex, the children never would have felt the sun warming their faces or the rain pelting their heads.

Solomon had grown accustomed to brothel life. The agonizing screams and haunting laughter no longer gave him nightmares. He was living in a man-made hell, but he didn't know anything different. If not for his mother's stories, he would have assumed the entire world was a dungeon run by tyrants like Sir.

"I promise—someday you will have a better life," Hema repeatedly told him. But to herself, she asked, *Who will take care of Solomon if something happens to me? Who will care for him when he is sick?*

Hema had kept another secret from Sir: she hadn't told him Solomon was ill. Frequently the boy was too weak to crawl out from under the bed when his mother entertained clients. Instead he lay there in silence, laboring for every breath. Solomon grew worse—Hema had no choice but to risk retribution and seek Sir's permission to take him to a doctor.

"No," Sir replied flatly. "You will not leave the compound together."

"Will you allow one of the other girls to take him," Hema begged.

"No, he will live or die here."

Desperately she said, "But what if the others get the illness and it hurts your business?"

Sir's face tightened. "Take him to a doctor, but if he does not get well soon ..."

"Thank you," Hema said.

"Go, before I change my mind," he growled. "And if you run away, I will find you and kill both of you."

Hema lowered her head. "I understand."

DOCTOR VISIT

After visiting the doctor, Hema was relieved to learn that Solomon's condition was treatable, although it would take some weeks for him to fully recover.

A few days later, before receiving her first client of the day, Hema was notified she had a visitor at the front door. Joan, a caregiver from Project Rescue, had come to deliver some good news.

Joan grabbed Hema's hands and held them warmly. "We have talked to the brothel owner and he is releasing you into our care."

Hema's smile quickly faded into a frown. "But, why would he let us go?"

"We have been negotiating with him for some time," Joan said. "He said your son was sick and bad for business."

Hema's smile returned. She had failed to report to Sir that Solomon's condition was improving. "Where will we live and how will we eat?" she asked.

"For now, you and your son will come and live at Project Rescue. There you will learn a trade and start a new life," Joan said.

"When can we go?" Hema asked.

"The brothel owner said he needed two weeks to replace you."

Hema threw her arms around Joan and whispered in her ear. "Thank you for everything."

Joan whispered back, "Thank Jesus—He has made this happen for you."

Hema nodded.

"Be safe," Joan said. "I will come to get you in two weeks."

Hema's face glowed as she raced off to tell Solomon.

Word of Hema's release spread throughout the brothel. Some girls begged her privately to take them with her, but such chatter was reckless. Hema knew the pain Sir's fists could inflict.

Hema trembled as she heard Sir's distinctive steps approaching her cubicle. And, by the scowl on his face, she knew her fears were justified. Without warning, his open hand collided against her cheek and she fell awkwardly onto the bed.

"Get to your feet," he shouted profanely.

Hema was too dazed to respond.

"Do as I say," he barked.

Hema rolled over and caught a glimpse of the fire that raged in his eyes.

Slapping her again and again, he tore off her clothes and threw himself on top of her unresponsive body.

After brutalizing Hema, he chuckled. "You're not going anywhere—I still have plans for you."

Writing in pain, tears flowed down Hema's face. *Jesus,
please don't let Him do this to me anymore,* she prayed silently.
Please make a way for me to go to the Project Rescue Home of Hope.

Two weeks passed and Hema was still unsure of her
fate. She didn't know if Sir had indeed changed his mind or if
he was merely blowing off steam. She was afraid to ask. Besides,
one of the madams said he had fallen ill and would be away for
several weeks. All Hema could do was hope and pray that Joan
would come to her rescue.

THE DEPARTURE

Finally, like an angel sent from heaven, Joan summoned
Hema and Solomon to the front door.

Hema and Joan embraced. Little Solomon joined the
reunion by wrapping his arms around their thighs.

"This is the day," Joan said.

Hema knew what that meant: she had been prostituted
for the last time; she and her son were about to begin a new life
at Project Rescue.

"I don't know how to thank you," Hema whispered. "I
was afraid my owner had changed his mind."

Joan shook her head. "No, but I'd recommend that we
leave before he does."

Hema understood. Without collecting their meager

belongings, she and Solomon followed Joan to the car and set out for their new home.

God's timing was perfect. Moments later, a pale, gaunt Sir arrived at the brothel.

"Where is Hema?" he asked in a croaky voice.

"She and her son just left," a madam stammered.

Sir raised his hand as if to slap her, but he was too weak.

"I never was going to let them go," he snapped. "Never."

"Do you want me to have someone find her and bring her back?" the madam asked.

Sir coughed and weighed his answer. "No," he finally said. "Her son is ill and she is reading the Bible—neither is good for business."

Though Uncle had

no knowledge of her

whereabouts, for many nights

she had nightmares of him

materializing at her door and

taking out his vengeance on

her and her son.

CHAPTER 3

VALERIE

The air was crisp and the sky a gloomy gray. But, for 12-year-old Valerie, every day was dark and depressing. She had grown weary of the 14-hour days—roaming the streets, pleading with pedestrians. "Please, can you help me? I need something to eat," she had said a thousand times.

She had grown tired of the lies, too. Every penny she collected was passed on to her "keeper," a middle-aged man she called "Uncle." At the end of the day, as long as she brought him money, he would feed her and give her a warm bed. On bad days, a beating was her compensation.

Valerie's mother sold her into slavery when she was eight. At first, Uncle showered her with gifts and special attention. Life was easier under his watchful eye. But, on Valerie's 12th birthday everything changed. That night Uncle led Valerie into his bedroom, locked the door, and sexually assaulted her. After that night, her tears came easily. Feeling dirty and ashamed, anger raged beneath her emotions. Her body trembled every time he touched her. Fearing for her life, she loathed him in secret.

Whenever she entertained thoughts of running away, Uncle's cruel words and venomous threats would race through her mind: "I will kill you," he said, "if you try to leave me." *Even if I could escape*, she thought, *I have no place to go.*

As gray skies gave way to nightfall, Valerie hunkered down under a storefront window. But her respite was short lived.

"You need to move along," a police officer demanded.

Valerie looked up at the youthful officer. His shirt collar was two sizes too big, and his high-pitched voice betrayed inexperience. Even so, she was in no position to negotiate.

"You really can't sit here," he said.

Valerie rose to her feet. She was much taller and prettier than the police officer had first noticed.

"Are you alone?" he asked.

"No, I live with my 'Uncle'," she said.

"What are you doing out here?"

"Just wasting time."

"Don't you have a boyfriend or someone who watches out for you?"

"No boyfriend."

The police officer placed his hand on her shoulder.

"You know, I can watch out for you."

Valerie acted ignorant of his advances, but she knew what he was after.

"I must go," she said, dashing down the street without glancing back.

THE BEDROOM

In the months that followed, Valerie went to great lengths to elude the police officer. But she couldn't avoid Uncle's sexual attacks. Night after night, she sat in her bedroom in front of a small, cloudy mirror, preparing herself for his visit. She applied lipstick and combed her thick, black hair under a lone light bulb that dangled from the ceiling. For such a large and gaudy home, it lacked many basic amenities.

Her door swung open.

"Are you ready?" Uncle asked.

"Yes."

"Tonight you will be with someone else," Uncle said. "He asked for you. Make it a special night for him and I will do something nice for you."

Minutes later, the young police officer entered her room. With a boyish grin and the leering eyes of a man twice his age, he summoned Valerie to the bed and had his way with her.

Over the next few years, Uncle would open Valerie's

door to many more customers. As a result, she no longer begged for coins in the streets; instead, she pleaded for pity and gentleness in her bedroom.

At 16, Valerie discovered she was pregnant. She hid the news from Uncle as long as she could, fearing he would demand an abortion. Fortunately he let the baby live when Valerie pled repeatedly for him to have mercy.

But, one night, several years later, Uncle erupted in anger at Valerie's son. Rather than hit the boy, he took out his vengeance on Valerie, nearly beating her to death. "We don't need a child here," he yelled, alcohol slurring his words. "We have too many mouths to feed."

Valerie knew she had to escape—or risk certain death for her and her son. For months she contemplated her options.

One day her answer came with a knock at her door.

"Are you Valerie?" the woman asked.

"Yes."

"I am Officer Catherine. It was reported to us that you and your child are not living under acceptable circumstances."

The officer read the fear in Valerie's eyes. "You do not have to be afraid anymore," she said. "We want to take you from this place."

"What about Uncle?" Valerie asked.

"He's being held. He will no longer bring you harm. But, come, we must hurry."

Valerie's eyes flitted from side to side, as if contemplating her future. She froze momentarily. *What if Uncle finds me? What will he do to me and my son?*

"Please, gather your things. Let us help you," the officer said.

Sensing this might be her last chance at freedom, Valerie leapt into action.

A NEW HOME

Days later, Valerie and her son arrived at their new home, a counseling facility affiliated with Project Rescue. Though Uncle had no knowledge of her whereabouts, for many nights she had nightmares of him materializing at her door and taking out his vengeance on her and her son.

Sharma, a caregiver at the home, befriended Valerie and her son.

"Why are you so kind to us?" Valerie asked Sharma.

"We love you and so does Jesus—that's why."

"Why would Jesus love me?"

"He loves all of us. He died for us."

Sharma could almost anticipate the myriad of questions racing through Valerie's mind. She explained how Jesus had died on a cross for her sins and, after three days, rose again. And she shared about His love and mercy and His gift of eternal life.

Valerie listened intently. "This is all new to me," she said. "How can I know this is true?"

"As you read the Bible I gave you," Sharma said, "Jesus will confirm in your heart that He loves you and that He is real."

As the weeks passed, Valerie made many new friends who nurtured her and her son back to health. They were laughing and playing again. They had found a home where they could sleep in a warm bed and awaken each morning to a nutritious meal. For the first time, they had nothing to fear. They were safe and secure.

But one day Valerie burst into Sharma's office holding a letter. Somehow Uncle had located her and was threatening to bring her home.

"I must leave," Valerie said, with terror in her voice. "If I stay here I'm afraid of what Uncle will do."

"Where would you go?" Sharma asked.

"Uncle says he will stop drinking and not harm me or my son. It will be different this time."

"We can't force you to stay, but please make sure you're doing the best thing for you and your son," Sharma pleaded. She had seen women escape abusive relationships before, only to return to their tormenters and more violence.

"If you return to Uncle and find that things haven't changed, will you please come back?" Sharma begged. "Do not be afraid to call me if you need my help."

Valerie nodded. She knew the risk but wanted to give Uncle a chance at redeeming himself.

The two women embraced and prayed together, but Sharma feared Valerie was walking into a trap of sorts. She couldn't bear to imagine her friend being prostituted or beaten again. But now all she could do was pray.

THE RETURN

Months later, Sharma's phone rang early one morning.

"Miss Sharma," Valerie announced.

"Valerie!" Sharma cheered. "I've been wondering how you were doing."

"I need help," Valerie said, her voice breaking. "Uncle hurt me and threatened my son."

"Valerie, your home is with us," Sharma said.

"I'm sorry I didn't listen to you, Miss Sharma."

"You wanted Uncle to change."

"He wanted me to give myself to other men. When I refused, he ...."

"God doesn't expect you to stay there," Sharma interrupted.

"I want to come back."

"Where are you? We will pick you up."

"I'm on the side of the road, near the market."

"Stay there. We will find you," Sharma said.

"Miss Sharma, I need a doctor," Valerie said.

"What's wrong?"

"Uncle hit my head—I'm bleeding."

"Wrap your wound and do not move. Is your son safe?"

"Yes, but frightened."

"We're on our way."

"Come quickly, Miss Sharma," Valerie implored.

Valerie's son was hovering over his mother's prone body when Sharma and the doctor arrived.

"Valerie, this is Sharma. Can you hear me?"

The doctor removed the makeshift bandage and shook his head. The wound was deep and Valerie was fading in and out of consciousness.

"We must get her to a hospital," he said.

"Let's get her to the car," Sharma ordered.

Valerie's son was crying as the car sped away.

"Your mama will be all right," Sharma said, turning to glance at the boy.

The doctor peered at Sharma as if he wasn't so sure.

"She has to make it," Sharma declared.

"We need to pray," the physician whispered. "This does not look good."

Without skipping a beat, Sharma broke into a prayer: "Jesus, please help Valerie. Help us get to the hospital in time."

Sharma held back her tears—trying to remain strong for the boy.

"Where am I?" Valerie asked, unexpectedly coherent. "Where is my son?"

"He's right here. This is Sharma—we are taking you to the hospital."

"Am I ...?" Valerie slurred.

"Save your strength," Sharma said.

"Jesus, I need Your help," Valerie prayed faintly.

"He is with you, Valerie," Sharma said.

"I know ... I can feel Him...."

Valerie suddenly faded.

"Jesus, help her hold on," Sharma cried.

At any moment, she feared the doctor would report he had lost her pulse. *What will I tell her boy?* Sharma asked herself. Finally the doctor broke a long silence. "Miss Sharma—something has happened."

"What?" she asked, her voice shaking.

"I don't understand—her pulse is getting stronger," he said.

"What does that mean?"

"I think it means she's going to make it," he announced.

Like a dam breaking, tears of joy gushed down Sharma's cheeks. Her prayer had been answered.

Sharma didn't know what the future held for Valerie, but she couldn't help but think that God had something special in mind. After all, He had certainly gone to great lengths to rescue her from the clutches of the evil one ... again.

For the next 20 years, Dana

was prostituted, beaten and

tortured. The memory of her

brothers' faces had almost

faded, but it was the hope of

seeing them again that kept

her alive.

CHAPTER 4

DANA

Dana stirred awake and squinted at the morning sun. The 8-year-old couldn't help but feel sorry for her pregnant mother, who had departed two hours earlier—when it was still dark—to work in the family's small rice paddy. Dana would have given anything to work alongside her mother, but her parents said the paddy was no place for a young girl. Besides, they said, they needed her to care for her baby brother, Ali.

That morning Dana finished her chores before mounting Ali on her back for the long trek to the village watering hole. After setting Ali on the soft bank, Dana gathered her knapsack filled with dirty clothes and a small bar of soap, and knelt in the water nearby.

Ali began to cry, but that quickly subsided when Dana hummed his favorite melody. He just needed to hear her voice.

"Ali, we'll go swimming soon," she said. "I just need to lay the clothes on the rocks so they can dry in the sun."

Already, Dana displayed motherly skills beyond her age.

As she studied her reflection in the murky water, Dana replayed her conversation with her mother the night before. "You're a beautiful girl, Dana," her mother said. "Someday you'll be a good wife and mother." Rubbing her stomach, she added, "And soon you'll be taking care of the new baby."

Dana smiled confidently, welcoming the challenge. But little did she know what was lurking around the corner for her and her siblings.

As far as Dana could remember, her mother had never been sick. At least she hadn't missed a day of work. Even after her brother David was born, her mother was back to work in a matter of days. So, Dana knew it was serious when her mother didn't have the strength to get out of bed.

One morning, weeks later, Dana attempted to wake her mother by stroking her cheek. But her skin was cold and her body lifeless—she had died in her sleep.

Dana's life changed that day. Besides caring for Ali and the newborn baby, now she was required to spend her days cooking, collecting water and firewood, and keeping the family's hovel in order. Meanwhile her father was forced to work longer hours in the paddy fields.

ALL ALONE

As time passed, and the two boys were able to handle

simple chores, Dana began to work alongside her father. *Mother was right*, Dana told herself, *the paddy was no place for a young girl*. But her tenure in the fields would be short lived. One night, when her father did not return for dinner, Dana braved the moonlit darkness to find him.

"Papa!" she hollered. "Papa, can you hear me? Papa!"

There was no response.

"Papa! Papa!" she yelled, circling the paddy.

Finally her eyes fell on her father—his body was face down in the water. Rolling him over, immediately she knew he was dead. Tears cascaded down her face and panic set in. Now she had no one left. Horrifying questions rushed in: *What will happen to me and my two brothers? How will we live? Who will tend to the paddy?*

Dana's fears were justified. At first, villagers provided food and other assistance. But, within weeks, Dana knew they were on their own. And there was no way she could farm the paddy alone. With nowhere to turn, the three siblings resorted to begging in the market. They learned quickly how to tug on the heartstrings of villagers and the best places to panhandle tourists.

"Come here, little girl," a well-dressed man said. "I have some money for you and some bread, too, if you will help me."

Dana followed him to a nearby hut. The man proceeded to kiss and rape her, claiming, "If you scream, I will not give you the money."

For Dana, the pain was unbearable. She wanted to die—but all she could do was close her eyes and cry.

"What is your name?" the man asked, yanking up his trousers.

Her voice quivering, she said, "Dana."

"Dana, here is the money I promised."

The sight of so much money helped to numb her pain.

"I will be back in several weeks," he said. "If you will come with me, I will give you more money."

Lifeless and emotionally broken, she nodded. She knew the money in her hand would feed her and her two brothers for a week.

A month later, the man steered his car alongside the young girl and rolled down his window. "Dana, will you spend some time with me today? I have more money for you."

Dana hesitated.

"I won't hurt you," he said. "I just want to help you."

Reluctantly, she entered the car.

That was the last time anyone in the village would see her.

As the car sped from the village, Dana asked, "Where are we going?"

"I'm taking you to the city," he said flatly.

"What for?"

"I am going to buy you a dress," he said. "Does that make you happy?"

Sensing danger, she didn't answer immediately.

"My brothers are expecting me," she said.

"You will be back very soon," he promised.

Two hours later, the car maneuvered through a city maze, finally arriving at a dilapidated building.

"Come—this is it," he snapped.

"What is this?"

"They call it a brothel—and this is your new home."

"I must return to my brothers," Dana demanded.

Before she could utter another word, the man grabbed the back of her neck and threw her to the ground. "This is your home—this is your new life," he growled.

TWENTY YEARS

For the next 20 years, Dana was prostituted, beaten and tortured. The memory of her brothers' faces had almost faded, but it was the dream of seeing them again that kept her alive. *Someday I will find them*, she told herself. *Mama would want me to make sure they are well.*

In time, however, Dana's resilience would be tested. She couldn't help it—the burns and bruises on her arms provoked thoughts of suicide.

Just when she thought she couldn't survive another day,

a social worker came to Dana's aid. The woman convinced the brothel owner to permit Dana to attend the Project Rescue vocational training center a few hours each day. After all the years of torment and ridicule, her breakthrough had finally come.

Project Rescue became Dana's sanctuary—a place where no one could bring her harm. There, she also met Cora, a caregiver who always seemed to have the right words.

The first time Cora heard Dana's story, she wept as if they were sisters. Dana had never witnessed such empathy and compassion.

"People tell me I'm beautiful," Dana said to Cora. "But they cannot see the holes in my heart."

"God knows how to heal your hurts," Cora said.

"I can't describe what men have done to me," she said. "The only way I could ever believe in God is if He helped me leave the brothel and find my family."

"All I know is that God can do impossible things," Cora said.

Over the next few years, Dana and Cora conversed almost daily about the mysteries of God. As their trust in one another grew, Dana confided stories of the brutality that had left scars on her body.

"God is with you," Cora said. "Don't give up."

But Dana had experienced too many disappointments to allow hope to linger very long. For now, she could endure long nights at the brothel if her days could be spent at Project Rescue.

Over time, Dana learned to read and write and developed skills as a seamstress. When Cora began showing Dana's work to local merchants, they began placing orders for her clothing. "I'll buy everything she makes," one shop owner said.

Dana was leaning over her sewing machine one day, when Cora ran toward her with an envelope in hand.

"God has answered our prayers, Dana," she said. "He has given you your freedom."

"Miss Cora, what are you saying?"

"This is a letter from the brothel owner granting your release. One of the merchants paid him so you could produce more clothing. What I'm saying is ... you are free."

Her hands trembling, Dana reached for the letter and began reading behind a waterfall of tears.

"I never thought this day was possible," Dana said.

"God rescued you, Cora."

"Yes, I believe He did."

The two women wrapped their arms around one another and squeezed tight. They knew they had just witnessed a miracle.

REUNITED

Eventually Dana moved out of the vocational center to begin her new life. Years earlier, her brothers had been adopted and taken to places unknown. There was no need to return to the village of her childhood, where she would be forced to relive ghastly memories. So, Dana settled in a village near the vocational center, where she could help other women overcome the pain of sexual slavery.

Upon arriving home from an afternoon at the vocational center, Dana found a well-dressed young man waiting at her door. His perfectly styled hair and engaging smile told Dana he meant her no harm.

"Is your name Dana?" he asked.

"Yes," she replied anxiously. "May I help you?"

"You are new here," he stated.

"Yes, I just moved here."

"I have lived here for many years," he said.

"How did you know my name?" she asked.

"Well, someone in the village mentioned that your name was Dana. That was the name of my sister, but we were separated when we were very young."

"What is your name?" Dana asked.

"They call me Ali."

"Ali?" Dana cried.

Taking the young man's face in her hands, Dana stared

into his eyes to see if it could be true.

"My brother and I have been searching for you all these years," he said.

"And it took God in heaven to bring us back together," she declared.

The two siblings simply cried in each other's arms, letting their tears of joy do their talking.

Breaking the silence, Dana said, "There's so much I want to tell you."

Ali smiled and wiped the tears from his eyes. "Well, now we have all the time in the world."

Vela was at an age when

brothel owners prostituted

children. Thousands of young

girls adorned in colorful saris

spent their days soliciting

men in the streets.

CHAPTER 5

VELA

Motorized rickshaws, overcrowded buses, dented taxis and smog-belching autos jockeyed on the streets of the red-light district. Had it not been for their mission, Sonya and her co-worker, Sam, would have chosen to brave these streets at a less combative hour.

"We had no choice but to come now," Sonya said. "When we get calls like this one, we have to move quickly."

Sam nodded his head, attempting to dodge potholes.

"I've never gotten used to coming down here," Sonya said.

"Hopefully we'll be able to retrieve the girl quickly ... and get out without any problems," Sam said.

"Hopefully," Sonya repeated. But Sonya was a bundle of nerves—removing a child from the brothels was no easy task.

Sonya had met Vela and her mother, Nileen, a year ago, but she had lost contact with them when they moved to a different brothel. So, Sonya was surprised to receive a call from

Nileen, requesting that she collect Vela and take her to
the ministry home.

As their car pulled up to the brothel—nothing more
than a collection of shanties—Sonya and Sam could see young
girls peering from behind the soiled curtains.

Turning off the ignition, Sam said, "God be with us."

Nileen, a petite woman with a demanding voice, met
them on the street.

"Please, follow me," she said. "We can't talk here."

Guiding them down a narrow path between the hovels,
Nileen turned and whispered, "Wait here and I will get Vela."

Moments later, Vela appeared through a slit curtain.
Her eyes fixed on the ground and her lip turned up, the 8-year-
old resembled a child boarding the bus for her first day
of school.

"Vela," Nileen said flatly. "It's time for you to go with
Miss Sonya. We must move quickly."

Sonya understood Nileen's trepidation: Vela was at an
age when brothel owners prostituted children. Thousands of
young girls adorned in colorful saris spent their days soliciting
men in the streets. *It's good that Vela is leaving now*, Sonya said
to herself. *With her high cheekbones and pearl-like skin, she could
earn the brothel owners a handsome profit.*

There were no farewell tears or goodbye hugs between
Nileen and Vela. Instead, a robotic Vela followed Sonya and
Sam to their car and climbed inside.

Sam glanced at Sonya as he turned the key. "So far, so good," he said.

"Vela," Sonya said from the front seat, "it's good to see you again. You have become such a beautiful girl."

Vela, her chin pressed against her chest, didn't move a muscle or utter a word.

"Would you like some water?" Sam asked.

Lost in her thoughts, Vela gave no reply.

Sonya shot Sam a look as if to say, *She'll talk when she's ready—no need to force it.*

Sonya tucked Vela into bed and sat beside her that first night in the home. "I know you're scared ... and I know you miss your family. But, this is the best place for you. Do you believe that?"

The child peered into Sonya's eyes, as if trying to read her intentions.

"Did you get enough to eat?" Sonya asked. "Are you feeling better?"

Vela nodded slightly.

"Good. Well, I want you to sleep well tonight. Tomorrow morning you're going to meet your teacher and make some new friends."

With a light pat on the child's head, Sonya withdrew to the kitchen for a cup of tea. The house was unusually quiet— even for this late hour—the perfect time to make an entry in her journal. Writing wasn't particularly enjoyable for Sonya, but it had proven to be therapeutic. Unmarried and professionally focused, Sonya was fortunate to have the team at Project Rescue as her family. She had committed her life to helping prostituted women and their children. But, dealing with so much emotional pain and heartache often left her empty by the end of the day. Writing in her journal helped her gain perspective. Often, tears would drip onto the pages as God spoke to her heart and gave her words of encouragement.

Journal Entry: May 14

We picked up Vela today at the brothel without a hitch. On the way back to the home, she vomited all over the back seat. I'm sure it was part nerves and part car sickness. But it's fulfilling to know that we played a part in rescuing another girl from the brothel. Every time we go there, I see so many women and children who need our help. I pray that Nileen finds a way out of the brothel soon. I know she will pay a price for sending us her daughter. When the brothel owners find out, they may beat her. God, please protect her tonight ... and thank you for giving Vela a new life.

Vela rubbed her eyes and crawled out of bed. The five girls sharing her room had already dressed themselves and eaten a bowl of hot cereal.

"Good, you're awake," Sonya said. "I found a dress that's just about your size ... and some new shoes to go with it. Go ahead—try them on and I'll be right back."

When Sonya returned a few minutes later, the pile of clothes remained untouched.

"What's the matter, Vela?" Sonya asked.

Vela peered up without a word.

"Do you need me to help dress you?"

Vela nodded.

Buttoning the dress, Sonya said, "Now, go look at yourself in the mirror."

Vela studied the reflection of herself as Sonya peered over her shoulder.

"Now, that's one pretty little girl," Sonya exclaimed.

Vela cracked a smile. "Thank you," she said, fixed on the mirror.

Finally Sonya had to pull the child away—so she could eat breakfast and attend class. But a big grin materialized on Sonya's face. She knew she had just witnessed a breakthrough: Vela was talking and smiling.

Journal Entry: July 21

It's hard to believe Vela has been with us two months. It's taken a lot more time than I thought for her to adjust to life outside the brothel. But I guess it's understandable that she put up walls around herself—given the abuse that she faced as a child. We completed her educational testing and it was no surprise that Vela is like most of the kids raised in brothels—she's far behind. Hopefully she'll work hard and be able to catch up. I received word that Nileen wants to visit Vela. I'm concerned that this might set Vela back, but there's really nothing we can do if she shows up at our front door.

Sonya watched from across the kitchen as Vela stood over a pot of lamb curry and stirred it intently with a large wooden spoon. Around her, three young girls huddled close.

"You must stir it as it cooks," Vela told them, "or you will burn the pan."

"Can I try?" one girl asked.

Vela placed the spoon in the girl's hand and guided it in circles around the pot. The scene brought a smile to Sonya and Sam's faces. They were equally pleased by Vela's progress in the classroom. In particular, her teachers marveled at her accelerated growth in math and reading.

"There's something special about Vela," Sonya told Sam. "If she stays close to God, she has a bright future ahead of her."

"She's always among the first to complete her afternoon chores," Sam said. "She's come a long ways in a short time."

Their conversation was cut short by a knock at the door.

Sonya swung the door open.

"Nileen," Sonya announced. "It's so good to see you."

"Thank you," Nileen said, placing her palms together. "May I see Vela."

"Yes, please have a seat and I will bring her to you," Sonya said.

"Good. I must talk to you as well," Nileen said.

Moments later, Sonya returned with Vela.

"You have grown," Nileen said, without embracing her daughter.

"Isn't she beautiful?" Sonya added. "She's one of our best students—very smart."

Nileen smiled and spoke directly to Vela. "I have some news: your brother is getting married and he wants you to live with him."

Vela recoiled.

"But she's doing so well here," Sonya implored.

"Yes, but her family needs her," Nileen demanded.

Sonya feared that leaving Project Rescue could make Vela vulnerable again to brothel owners and sex-traffickers. "Please, do what's best for Vela," she implored.

"That's exactly what I'm doing," Nileen countered. "Vela, get your things—we are leaving."

Torn and confused, Vela hesitated.

Everything within Sonya wanted to ask the child where she wanted to live, but she knew that wasn't appropriate. Nileen was still her mother. Sonya knew her hands were tied.

Journal Entry: October 14

> I am crying as I write these words. Today I watched Vela leave the home. I know she wanted to stay, but there was nothing more I could do. I know God is in control, but I don't understand how anything good can come out of this. She was growing in so many ways, including her faith. Now, we don't know what will happen to her. She's such a beautiful girl, but I'm afraid she may have a tragic future. Why did it have to end this way? Why did she have to leave? I'll never forget how she looked back at me, her eyes pleading for my help. I'm afraid that moment will haunt me for the rest of my life. All I can do now is pray … and hope that one day Nileen calls me again to come and pick up her precious little girl.

She was oblivious to the

dangers lurking around her.

Men eyed her lustfully, as if

she were 10 years older.

C H A P T E R   6

R E V I

Ten-year-old Revi nipped at her mother's stilettos down trash-laden alleys to a bustling street corner.

"Stay here," Mama ordered. "I'll come and get you later."

From her perch in a department store entryway, Revi watched Mama wade into a sea of blaring taxis, black-belching trucks and expensive sports cars. Flashing her legs to would-be customers, she climbed inside one automobile after another.

Revi was determined to earn money, too.

"Please, Mister," she said, extending an empty cup toward a beleaguered businessman.

Shoving his hand in his pocket, he deposited a few coins into her cup.

"Thank you, Mister," Revi said with a grin. Although she had grown accustomed to rejection, on a good night, she "earned" enough to feed herself.

Nevertheless, she was oblivious to the dangers lurking around her. Men eyed her lustfully, as if she were 10 years older.

Some offered money if she would accompany them to a seedy motel, but Mama made her promise never to leave her nesting place.

Mama warned her daughter not to talk to policemen or social workers. "They will take you from me," she said.

Revi feared a woman named Linda might actually be a social worker, so she didn't tell Mama about the food the woman dropped off from time to time.

"Hi, Revi," Linda said with a sincere smile.

"Hi."

"I brought you some fruit and a bottle of water," Linda said.

Revi peeled an orange and tasted the juice exploding in her mouth.

"It's good, huh?" Linda asked.

The child nodded.

"Revi, I have talked to your guardian—your grandmother," Linda said. "She would like you to come and live at our home for girls for a while. It's up to you, but you'll have your own bed, clothes, food, and you'll get to learn and make many new friends. Would you like that?"

"Can Mama come, too?"

"Your mother says she isn't ready, but your grandmother thinks she will let you come."

Revi's face went blank. "We must ask Mama," she said.

"Yes, tomorrow we will talk to your mama," Linda said,

"and we'll ask her to give her blessing."

"... and ask her to come with me," Revi added.

"Yes, we will ask her again," Linda promised.

Revi's grandmother always said the moon was the eye of a god looking down on Earth. But the moon was no longer visible when Revi's mother finally collected her for the long trek home. *The god must be sleeping tonight*, the child told herself.

"Mama, look how much money I have," Revi said, handing her the cup.

Rolling her eyes, Mama snapped, "Tomorrow you must do better."

Hearing the strain in Mama's voice, Revi was afraid to tell her about Miss Linda's visit. Besides, the night had not been good to Mama: the left side of her face was bruised. Revi thought it best to just keep quiet and to walk at a safe distance behind her.

VISITORS

Usually noon church bells served as a wake-up call for Revi and her mother. But, this time they were awakened by a polite knock on their door.

Revi opened the door slowly to the smiling faces of her grandmother and Linda.

"Revi, is your mother here?" Linda asked.

"Yes, she's still sleeping," she replied.

"Then, go wake her up and tell her I am here," Revi's grandmother ordered.

Twenty minutes passed before a dazed Mama appeared, her hair resembling a ragged mop. "Why have you come at this hour?" she slurred.

Holding Revi to her side, the grandmother said, "This is Linda from Project Rescue and I have asked her to take Revi."

"Take her where?"

"To a home and school for children," Linda replied. "We'll give her an education and take good care of her for you."

"I don't want your help!" she argued.

"You can come, too," Revi said.

"Yes, we would love for you to come," Linda added.

"Neither of us are going with you," Mama said, pulling Revi away.

"I am her guardian," her grandmother said. "The court says it's my decision."

"I am her mother," Mama yelled.

Linda attempted to turn down the volume of their dispute. "You are her mother," she said calmly. "And, as her mother, I know you want what's best for Revi. Please ... let her come ... so she can learn to read and write."

Mama paused. She had always wanted to learn to read herself. Could she deny that privilege to her daughter?

"I need her," Mama said.

"Then come with her," Linda said. "We'll help you."

Ignoring Linda's invitation, Mama turned her assault on Revi's grandmother. "You have done this. You are taking Revi from me. I hate you! I will not let her go."

"You have no choice," the grandmother shot back. "I'll bring the police if I have to."

Mama had seen that stubborn look before. Descending into an old chair, she buried her face in her hands.

"Everything will be okay," Linda promised. "We'll arrange for you to come and see her."

"I will not ..." Mama said. "I will never see her again."

"Yes, I'll make sure of it," Linda said. "You have my word."

"If she walks out that door ..." Mama's voice trailed off.

Revi set her hand on her mother's shoulder, saying, "I will see you very soon."

Without looking up at her daughter, Mama finally nodded her approval.

JOY AND SADNESS

Months passed and Revi adjusted quickly to her new surroundings. She spent hours each day poring through books and learning to pronounce syllables. She loved to wade into the toy box and play "tag" outside with the other children. For the first time in her life, she felt safe and valued. But underneath all the joy was a measure of sadness, because her mother had not come to visit her. She wanted to show off her reading skills and introduce her to her teachers and playmates.

"Miss Linda," Revi asked. "Why hasn't my mama come to see me?"

"This has been a hard time for her," Linda said. "But I'll do my best. If she could see you now, I know she'd be so proud and happy."

Revi said, "Mama has had a hard life. I dreamt last night that she came to live with me.".

"We would love for that to happen, too," Linda said. "Keep praying."

That night, Revi knelt by her bed and asked Jesus to help her mother. She could hear the harsh rain pummeling the window and knew nights like this weren't good for Mama's business. "Dear Jesus," she said. "I don't know where Mama is and I miss her, but please bring her to Project Rescue. She doesn't know You like I do. She doesn't know You love her. She's all alone—she needs Your help."

Four months passed and Revi's mother had not paid her a visit. Nevertheless, Revi refused to lose hope. She kept praying—and asked her teachers and playmates to pray, too.

But Linda was unusually formal when she entered Revi's room one night. Immediately Revi knew something was wrong.

"Revi, come and sit on my lap," Linda said. "I know

you've been praying for your mother for a long time. I've been praying, too. Yesterday, I went to her house and she wasn't there. So, at night, I went to the street corner and she wasn't there either."

"Where is she?" Revi interrupted.

"Well, they told me she went to work in another city, for more money."

"What city?"

"No one knows where she went—not even your grandmother."

"Is she okay?"

"I'm sure she's okay," Linda replied, though fearing the worst.

"What can we do to help her?"

"All we can do is pray," Linda said.

Revi's faith remained strong. "Jesus helped me—I know He's going to help Mama, too."

Linda pulled the young girl tightly to her chest and kissed the crown of her head. She didn't have the heart to tell her the truth: Her mama had fallen in with some powerful traffickers, and without a miracle it was unlikely the child would ever see her mama again.

She felt more like his

prisoner than his daughter.

The 17-year-old glanced back

at her mother and younger

sisters, who were swiping

tears from their cheeks, too.

CHAPTER 7

A B L A

Abla draped the scarf over her head to protect her braids from the rain. Grabbing her friend Moussa's hand, together they danced their way around puddles through the crowded, chaotic streets. But they both knew rain was just an excuse to hold hands—their religion forbade such public affection between men and women.

Hiding under a sun-faded awning, Moussa spun Abla around to plant a kiss. But she pulled away. "My father is waiting for me in the square," she said. The downpour suddenly slowed to a sprinkle and steam began rising from the streets.

"Come on," he said. They raced down an alley until Moussa knew it was time for him to disappear into the crowd. Abla didn't want her father to see them together, so she waved goodbye and scurried ahead.

"Hello, Father."

"Abla," he announced. His dark, bushy eyebrows narrowed as he measured her face. "I've made a decision about your future: I've sold you to a man named Qumar. Tomorrow you will become his possession."

"How could you do this?" she said angrily.

"It is what is best for the family," he shot back.

"I will run away before I do this," she threatened.

"Listen to me—it is done," he shouted, squeezing her arms until they bruised.

Two hours later, Abla collapsed onto her bed and stared emptily at the ceiling. She weighed her options: honor her father's wishes and live with a stranger ... or run away and never see her family again. The tears came easily and soaked her pillow. She prayed to the god of her family, but felt no one was listening. Finally she fell asleep—uncertain what the morning would bring.

That night she dreamt about her family: She saw them walking away from her, down a treacherous road where storms were raging. In her dream, she screamed, *Mother, Father, you're headed in the wrong direction*. But they wouldn't listen. Turning her head, her eyes were drawn to a different road—one that was peaceful, serene and more inviting. Then she heard a voice: *Abla, My name is Jesus. Trust in Me. I am the one true God. I will help you ... if you follow Me.*

The morning sunlight crossed Abla's face through a break in the curtain and her eyes snapped open. The dream seemed so real that tears surfaced. Then, as if drawn by a magnet, she flew out of bed, threw on some clothes, and raced out the door. She didn't have a destination; she just knew there was somewhere she needed to be.

Still reflecting on her dream, Abla wandered into a church with a statue of Jesus out front.

A short man with a kind voice appeared from nowhere. "May I help you?" he asked. "I'm Pastor Gimenez."

"Yes, my name is Abla and I have a question," she stuttered.

"I will try," he replied.

"Sir, this may not make any sense to you, but last night I had a dream and a Man named Jesus spoke to me," she said. "I need someone to help me understand what it means."

For nearly two hours, the pastor listened to Abla's story and answered her questions.

"Jesus loves you," he said. "He came to you in a dream because He wants you to follow Him."

Abla closed her eyes as if mustering courage. She knew her family would disown her—but she had to pursue what was true. "I am ready to follow Him," she replied. "What must I do?"

The pastor led Abla in prayer, asking Jesus to forgive her sins and to grant her the gift of eternal life. Instantly she felt the peace and warmth of Jesus' love.

When Abla returned home, her father rose to his feet and stiffened like a medieval sentry. "Abla, where have you been?" he yelled. "I demand to know!"

"Father, I have found a new direction for my life and I will not marry the man you have chosen," she said firmly.

Flames raged in her father. He grabbed her hair and pulled her face to within an inch of his. "I will cut your throat if you don't do what I say."

"Father," she screamed.

"I will deliver you to your new husband and he can do with you what he wants. Get your things together—now!"

Moments later, Abla's father shoved her into an old taxi and climbed in beside her. She felt more like his prisoner than his daughter. The 17-year-old glanced back at her mother and younger sisters, who were swiping tears from their cheeks, too.

WEDDING NIGHT

Had her family witnessed the torture she would endure her first night with Qumar, they never would have agreed to her marriage. Raped and beaten, Abla crawled to a sink and washed the blood from her face and hair. Meanwhile, Qumar fell asleep in a drunken stupor, his body sprawled across the entire bed. Abla wanted to puncture his chest with a knife, but opted to run far away.

Jesus, how can I follow You if You won't protect me, she prayed. *I want to believe You are real, but You must lead me away from here.*

Stealing a roll of money from Qumar's pants, Abla sneaked outside and, without looking back, began a sprint for her life. At the edge of town, she paid a stranger to ride in the back of his open-air truck. Abla was unsure where her journey would lead; she just knew she had to keep moving. Qumar could awaken at any time and give chase.

Crossing the desert, she slept in a convoy of trucks carrying goats and livestock to port. *I am still not safe*, she thought. *I must take a boat to another city—then Qumar and my father will not be able to find me.*

Afraid and exhausted, she finally landed in a European port and wandered into a detention center. But it was there that she met Joy, a caregiver for Project Rescue, who visited the center each week to extend a helping hand to women like Abla.

"My name is Joy," she said.

"I'm Abla."

"Where did you come from?" Joy asked.

"I traveled a long distance," she replied.

"What brought you here?"

Abla shook her head. "I don't know. I just had to leave. This is where my journey brought me."

"Are you hurt?" Joy asked.

Abla paused. "I have many hurts—some that can't be seen."

"Well, I know Someone who knows all your pain—and He wants to help you."

"Who can know the things that have been done to me?"

"Well, His name is Jesus."

Abla grinned slightly. "I know this Jesus. He came to me in a dream and told me to follow Him."

Joy reached into her bag and retrieved a Bible. "This is for you—it's a Bible. It will teach you more about Jesus."

Abla pulled the Bible to her chest as if protecting her most treasured possession.

THE QUESTIONS

Every time Joy entered the detention center, Abla peppered her with questions from the Bible.

"Will I see my family in heaven?"

"Heaven is only for followers of Jesus," Joy said. "If they choose to follow Jesus, they'll be there, too."

"They worship other gods," she said sadly. "But maybe Jesus will come to them in a dream, too."

"Jesus is working to bring everyone to salvation."

"I want to see Jesus again—even if it's in a dream," Abla said. "I need to talk to Him."

"Make no mistake, He's with you," Joy said. "No matter where life takes you, He will be by your side."

"Mama Joy, yesterday I was offered a good job. But, if I accept it, I must move away from this country. What would Jesus want me to do?"

Joy's smile faded. She learned long ago to distrust anyone who promised riches—especially in a foreign country. Too many girls had been lured into sexual slavery by reaching for the brass ring of "a better life."

"Do you trust me?" Joy asked.

"Yes, Mama—I trust you."

"Then don't take this job," she said. "It may take you down a dangerous road."

"Mama Joy, I have nothing to keep me here. A job will give me a new start. I want to do something with my life. I cannot stay at the detention much longer."

"Then come live at Project Rescue and help me care for other women who have been through much pain and disappointment."

"Mama Joy, I am so thankful to you. You have taught me. I'm alive again because of you. I would never do anything to disappoint you. But I must ask Jesus what to do."

"Yes, please pray. I know Jesus will show you the way."

The two women embraced like they had after many conversations. But this time Joy felt something ominous—as if a war were being waged for Abla's soul. Jesus needed her at Project Rescue, but the enemy wanted her to take a different road—one filled with heartache and lies.

Abla prayed herself to sleep that night: *God, I need You to show me what to do. I don't want to go anywhere or do anything unless I'm following You.*

Early the next morning Abla awoke to heavenly silence. The other residents in the center were still asleep, but Abla sensed she was in the presence of Jesus. She lay in bed with her eyes open and prayed silently:

Jesus, my father betrayed me and I still have much hatred in my heart toward him. Someday I know I must forgive him, but he has stolen my innocence and taken Moussa from me. How can I help other women deal with their pain at Project Rescue if I'm still dealing with my own problems?

As if Jesus had pulled up a chair next to her bed, Abla received the answers she had been seeking. She didn't hear an audible voice, but words formed in her mind as if Jesus were whispering in her ear:

Abla, you will never be perfect, but you are forgiven. Your healing will be complete as you help other women deal with their pain. Pursue obedience rather than opportunity. I saved you—now I want you to commit your life to saving others. I have led you every step of the way ... and I am calling you now to Project Rescue.

"Yes, Jesus," Abla replied quietly. "I have heard Your voice loud and clear—I'll dedicate my life to helping women just like me."

With a new calling on her life and peace in her heart, Abla closed her eyes and fell back asleep. That morning Jesus didn't return to her in a dream, but she knew He was guiding her down a path of no regrets.

Without responding, the woman clasped Rashmi's arm and dragged her back inside the hell of the brothel.

CHAPTER 8

RASHMI

The flowerpot shattered against the concrete wall, propelling ceramic shards, dirt and orchids in all directions.

"Rashmi!" Tasha demanded. "Stop! Please stop! You must control yourself."

Undeterred, the 10-year-old knocked over a table lamp and glared defiantly at Tasha, a caregiver at the girls home.

Tasha shook her head in frustration, weighing what course of action to take. She longed to comfort the child in her arms, but the tantrums were beginning to test everyone's patience.

Without warning, Rashmi bolted out the front door into the intense summer heat. Fine, red dirt filled the air around her bare feet as she ran off the property and onto the pockmarked road.

Rashmi had learned to run from her problems while growing up in the red-light district. Fleeing from men who preyed on her for sex was a daily ritual. But on this day, Rashmi was running from herself: her doubts, insecurities and fears.

"Richard, come quickly!" Tasha yelled. "Rashmi has run off again."

Richard, a Project Rescue worker in his late 20s, rolled his eyes. This wasn't the first time he'd been forced to track her down.

The girl's feet pounded the pavement like a drum beat. *This time I'm going to get away*, she thought.

Stopping to catch her breath, Rashmi glanced over her bony shoulder only to see a determined Richard gaining ground. She knew she couldn't outrun him—but she had to try.

Flying around the corner, Richard yelled, "Rashmi!"

Dropping her hands to her side, she pivoted to look Richard in the eye. "Let me go," she demanded.

Reaching out his hand, Richard said, "Come—let's go home."

Rashmi could hear the resolve in his voice and knew her race to nowhere had come to an end.

With a wide smile and a firm grip, Richard hoisted Rashmi onto his shoulder.

"When are you going to learn?" he asked with a kidlike chuckle. "We're your family now—we're going to take care of you."

Before arriving at Project Rescue, Rashmi had wallowed in neglect and abuse. Her mother died when Rashmi was 7, leaving the child alone to beg in the streets and scavenge for food in garbage heaps. That was her life until a woman with crooked teeth and a saggy throat adopted her into the brothel. There, Rashmi was forced to have sex with men old enough to be her father.

"You will do everything they tell you, Rashmi," the woman threatened, "or I will let them kill you. Do what I say—I am your mother now."

ON THE STREET

Rashmi was adorned in a colorful skirt, earrings and makeup—working for the brothel—when Richard and Tasha met her for the first time. While driving through the red-light district one day, they saw her soliciting men on a street corner.

"Look at that girl," Richard said. "She can't be any older than 10."

"Maybe younger," Tasha added.

Unexpectedly, Richard threw the Jeep into park and marched toward the child. From nowhere, a short, balding man with clumps of hair around his ears blocked his path.

"What do you want?" he asked.

Peering into the child's vacant eyes, Richard said, "I want you to let her go."

"Her mother pays me to watch over her," he snapped. "Move on or you will have to deal with me and my friends."

"I'll take my chances," Richard said confidently.

The man took a step closer and sneered at Richard. "This will not be good for you."

"She is coming with me," Richard insisted.

The man made a fist and shook it at Richard. "Leave while you can."

Richard stared back—even more determined. "I want you to take me to her mother."

"For what purpose?"

"I want to make her mother a business proposition."

The man thought for a moment: "What kind of proposition?"

"I want to pay her money," Richard replied.

"All right—follow me."

"Bring the girl, too," Richard demanded.

The brothel guard led Richard, Tasha and Rashmi across the street. "Wait here," he said, before disappearing through a door.

Moments later, Rashmi's "mother" appeared. Scowling at Richard and Tasha, she said, "What do you want with Rashmi?"

"We want to take Rashmi to a school."

The woman elevated her voice: "She doesn't need school. Get out of here."

"Don't you want Rashmi to be educated?" Tasha asked. "We have a home where she can learn to read. She'd be safe and have food to eat...."

"I don't care!"

"Are you really her mother?" Tasha asked.

Without responding, the woman clasped Rashmi's arm and dragged her back inside the hell of the brothel.

Richard and Tasha read the dedication in each other's eyes. *This is just the first chapter—this story isn't over,* they said to themselves. *God wants to rescue this child. We can't give up.*

A few days later, Richard and Tasha waited patiently outside the brothel until Rashmi and her "adoptive mother" took to the streets.

"May we talk to you?" Richard called at their backs.

Rashmi and her mother turned.

"What do you want?" the mother snapped.

"We want to give Rashmi a better life," Tasha replied. "As her mother, don't you want that for her?"

"She's not my mother," Rashmi replied awkwardly.

The woman recoiled and slapped the child's face. "I am the only mother you have," she hollered.

The picture was suddenly clearer for Richard and Tasha.

"We don't want to cause you trouble," Tasha said. "We just want to help Rashmi. With an education, she will one day make much more money."

"She can still live with you and come to school just a few hours each day," Richard added. "Please come and see it for yourself."

"Here's the address," Tasha said, handing her a piece of paper. "Come anytime."

The "adopted mother" nodded, but everyone knew she had no intention of letting Rashmi out of her sight. "I will consider it," she said, "but you must leave now."

Richard and Tasha smiled, cupped their palms together, and bowed out gracefully. They had learned long ago that prying children from the brothels was no easy task. It took time. And what was to be gained by backing the woman into a corner if they lost the fight for Rashmi's freedom?

Returning to their Jeep, Tasha said, "It will take an act of God for Rashmi to ever leave the brothel."

"Yes," Richard said. "She is making them too much money—but we can't give up. We've seen God do the miraculous before. We have to keep working and believing."

THE CONFESSION

Each week Richard and Tasha paid a visit to the woman claiming to be Rashmi's mother. Over time, she let her guard down and offered a confession: "She is not my daughter—I found her sleeping in a cardboard box," she said.

"Was she living alone when you found her?" Tasha asked.

"Yes, her mother had died," the woman replied. "When I found Rashmi, she was sickly, too."

"You saved her life," Richard lauded. "Would you now help us give her a better life?"

"The brothel will not allow it," she declared.

"We understand. But we will pray and ask our God to give you the courage to ask permission," Tasha said.

The woman bobbed her head, but a reddish shade of fear rose in her cheeks.

Several weeks later, the woman—with Rashmi in tow—stepped through the door of Project Rescue. Tasha came running to meet them as if reunited with long lost relatives.

"We're so glad you came—did you get permission?" Tasha asked excitedly.

Evading the question, the woman said, "She cannot return to the brothel, but I must go back immediately."

"Before you go, can we prepare you some food?"

"No. I must return," she said nervously.

Leaving no room for sentimental goodbyes, the woman darted out the door.

Tasha turned to greet Rashmi, but the child had crawled under a wooden table. She didn't know where she was—or what these strangers intended to do to her.

Peeling back the tablecloth and peering under the table, a smiling Tasha said, "Rashmi, you are going to live with us. When you're ready, we'll take you to your room."

Tapping her on the shoulder, Richard said, "Don't

worry—we'll earn her trust. We have to remember ... she's been exploited her entire life."

"I know one thing—she can't go back to the brothel," Tasha said. "I'm not sure they know she's here."

"Well, if they find out, they'll come looking for her," Richard said.

THE VISITOR

Weeks passed and, by all appearances, no one had earned a fleck of Rashmi's trust. Her tantrums and breakaways were frequent, her words mean-spirited. Years of abuse had left deep emotional scars. And Tasha was beginning to believe Rashmi was bruised and broken beyond her reach. *Only the hand of God can heal this child's mind and calm her fears,* Tasha told herself.

Late one night, a knock at the door sounded like a battering ram, waking up the residents. At the entrance stood a sophisticated man with designer shoes and a silk suit.

"May I help you?" Richard asked.

"You are hurting our business," the man said, his nostrils flaring. "You stop taking our girls or I will kill you."

Richard had faced this kind of threat before and knew exactly what to say: "Every child is here legally and with the government's blessing. If you want me to contact the authorities,

I'll have them here in an hour."

The visitor's eyes became like lasers. "You don't know who I am."

"I have their papers right here," Richard said. "The local authorities have placed them in our care and they're never going back to the brothel."

"You have no right to do this to my business," the man fired back.

"You have no right to do this to these children," Richard said, the hair rising on the nape of his neck.

"I want the child, Rashmi, to come with me!"

"Rashmi belongs here," Richard said forcefully. "She's part of our family now."

Little did Richard know that Rashmi had sneaked out of bed and was watching the confrontation from overhead. She heard every word as the two men engaged in a tug-of-war for her life. She trembled—her future was hanging in the balance.

Testing Richard's resolve, the man said, "Give me Rashmi ... or else."

"Rashmi stays here," Richard repeated.

The man glared into Richard's eyes as if testing his resolve. Then, like a vanquished boxer climbing out of a ring, the man turned and retreated down the steps to his luxury automobile.

Tiptoeing back to bed, remorse hit Rashmi like an Egyptian sandstorm. She regretted the times she ran away, the tantrums she threw, and the cruel words that spewed from her lips. *If it hadn't been for Richard*, she told herself, *tonight I would be back at the brothel ... or even dead*. It was the first time anyone had loved her enough to fight for her.

That night Rashmi drifted to sleep with a smile on her face. Finally she had a family to call her own.

Tears of shame surfaced in

Corinne's eyes. She knew

she'd never see Prita again

and she'd have to live

with the guilt of selling her

firstborn.

CHAPTER 9

PRITA

Corinne feared this dreadful day would come. She hadn't paid the rent for three months, and the landlord was coming to collect what he was due. Once again she'd have to surrender to his sexual advances or she'd be evicted.

"I see no end to my circumstances," Corinne confided to a neighbor. "Each month my debt is growing."

The neighbor—a man in his late 40s—moved closer as if to whisper a secret. "I know how you can change your situation."

"Tell me," Corinne said.

"People will pay a large sum for your oldest daughter— Prita."

Corinne took a step back. Though she would have aborted Prita if she'd had the money, she was grateful she'd brought the child full-term.

The neighbor continued to sell his solution. "One daughter is a small price to pay to help the entire family. Prita will be given a job and will be well taken care of."

"What kind of job?"

"She'd entertain wealthy men—and go to expensive places. You would be giving her a chance at a better life."

Corinne retreated. "I'll consider it."

The following day, she returned to her neighbor. "My rent must be paid; I will sell her."

"You won't be sorry," he said with a sly grin.

"I will be sorry; she's my daughter," Corinne snarled.

"They will come with the money tonight and receive her from you."

"She will be ready."

"You are doing the right thing."

"I hate what I must do," Corinne said under her breath. The neighbor nodded. He knew—as did Corinne—that 17-year-old Prita was not in store for a vacation or pleasure ride. She was about to endure unthinkable horrors in a city far away.

Tears of shame surfaced in Corinne's eyes. She knew she'd never see Prita again and she'd have to live with the guilt of selling her firstborn.

Sexual slavery was indeed cruel to Prita. After "entertaining" hundreds of men—and giving in to their twisted demands—she was angry and broken. Memories of anything good in her life had all but vanished.

When she finally escaped the brothel, local authorities

remanded her to the home run by Project Rescue. But the years of physical and emotional abuse made her transition to a different way of life difficult.

Night after night, Prita was content to lie in bed and converse with the demons in her head. She hated her mother and the men who had hurled her around like an unwanted toy. Although she didn't deserve their betrayal and abuse, the wounds of rejection were deep. Hostility spewed from her mouth like poison and, consequently, the other girls at Project Rescue sought to have her removed from the home.

"She is not respectful of anyone," said one of the girls.

"She doesn't want to be here," another said. "So why is she permitted to stay?"

"She's here because God sent her to us," the house parent said. "Be patient with her—God will deal with her in His time and in His own way."

The other girls weren't so sure: they had felt her scorn too many times. As far as they were concerned, she had already exhausted her chances—the home would be better off without her.

A NEW RESIDENT

No one could have dreamed that God would reach Prita through a new resident, 9-year-old Rachita, who had come to the home for a brief stay.

"What's your name?" Rachita asked.

"Prita," she replied without inflection in her voice.

"I'm Rachita."

"Why have they sent you here?" Prita asked dryly. "Most of us at this home are much older."

"I lived with my mama in the brothel—but she left. I was sent here until ..."

"I understand," Prita interrupted. "I was abandoned by my mother, too."

"Do you know where she is?" the girl asked.

"Yes, I think so. But I never want to see her again."

"I hope I see my mama. She left me, but she's still my mama."

"I have sisters your age," Prita said. "Someday I hope I will see them."

"Well, you can be my big sister," Rachita said.

A stoic Prita gave no response.

Months passed and local authorities had not found a permanent home for Rachita. So she and Prita spent many hours together, knowing that someday the child would be transferred to a government-run orphanage.

Rachita idolized Prita, but she knew to disappear when her "big sister" had an outburst of emotion. No one wanted to be near Prita when she was out of control.

But, to everyone's displeasure, Rachita was beginning

to follow in Prita's footsteps. One afternoon, the child lashed out at one of the Project Rescue caregivers, and was sent to her room.

"No, I won't go," Rachita rasped.

"Yes you will ... or you'll lose privileges," the worker said, firmly.

Rachita was defiant. "You don't own me," she yelled. Her tirades were even sounding like Prita.

One afternoon the caregivers huddled to express their concerns and seek a solution.

"As long as Rachita is here, we must teach her to respect authority," one worker said.

"Maybe we should separate Rachita and Prita," another said. "Prita has become a bad influence on all the younger girls."

The Project Rescue caregiver restated her position: "I still believe Prita will come around, but the local authorities may relocate Rachita any day. So, somehow we need to get through to that child before she's gone."

Reluctantly the caregivers nodded. They knew they needed God's help and an extra dose of patience.

A GOOD EXAMPLE

Prita tapped on Rachita's door and stepped inside. The child had already crawled into bed, but the lights were still on.

"Prita," Rachita called, her eyes wide open.

"I need to talk to you," Prita said flatly.

Rachita sat up in her bed.

Prita stroked the child's jet-black hair and stared into her dark eyes. "I came to tell you I am sorry," she said.

"What did you do?"

"I have not been a good example to you, little sister," Prita confessed. "I know I have many problems and sometimes I take it out on everyone around me. That is not the kind of person I want to be. And it's not the kind of person I want you to be."

"I'm sorry, too," Rachita said.

"We have to do better—do you promise?"

"Yes," the girl replied. "I will try harder."

"There's one more thing," Prita said. "I've been watching and listening: and there is something different about the workers here. They are so kind to us—even though we haven't always been kind to them."

Rachita listened intently.

"I want what they have," Prita said. "I want to know their God and ask Him to help me. And I want to live in heaven someday."

"How do we do that?" Rachita asked.

"They told me all I have to do is talk to their God, because He was listening," she replied. "They said I needed to ask Him to forgive me of my sins and believe that He sent His

Son Jesus to die on a cross."

"Can we do that before I go to sleep?" Rachita asked enthusiastically.

"I think we can, but only if you really want to."

Rachita smiled and nodded.

The two "sisters" held hands, closed their eyes, and prayed for the first time. Tears filled their eyes because they could sense God's presence and feel His healing power. They weren't sure what happened or where their newfound faith would take them. They just knew their lives would be better because God was now with them.

Throughout the night,

panic and uncertainty ruled

Nadia's thoughts. She vowed

to keep her eyes open until

morning for fear of the

hardened women sharing

her cell.

CHAPTER 10

NADIA

Though only 16, Nadia resembled a Parisian runway model: tall, slender and beautiful. She should have known that someone in the market would see her stealing the fruit. If she were caught, she knew the penalty would be severe. But, because she had not eaten all day, she plucked an apple from the pile and darted through the throng of shoppers.

"Stop!" she heard someone yell behind her. "Thief! Stop her. That one, the tall girl!"

Instantly angry vendors converged on her—like lions circling their prey. One spit on her. Another shoved her to the ground. The mob began to beat her with brooms and branches, evoking cheers from the crowd. Nadia covered her head to protect her face.

Finally a man stepped in. "Enough," he shouted. "That's enough." The beating stopped. The crowd disbursed.

"Can you walk?" the man asked, lifting her from the ground.

"Put your weight on me," he said. "I'll take you to a hospital."

"No," Nadia said, her vision blurred. "I just need to lay down."

That was the last thing Nadia remembered. Several hours later, she awoke on a couch in a strange home.

"Where am I?" she asked.

"You are at my home—how are you feeling?" her rescuer replied.

"I'm tired," she said.

"I think you have a concussion," the man said.

Nadia studied his face. By the wrinkles in his forehead, she estimated the guardian angel was in his 60s.

"Why did you steal?" he asked.

Nadia hesitated. "Because I was hungry."

"Where do you live—do you have a family?"

"I'm separated from my family."

"Where do they live?" he asked.

"Far from here," she said uncomfortably.

"Well, you can stay here with my wife and me until you are feeling better."

Nadia nodded. "Thank you. But why are you helping me?" she asked.

"We're followers of Jesus," he said. "We're just doing what He would do."

To Nadia, Jesus was tied to religious rituals and

holidays. She had never heard the story of His manger birth or His death on the cross. She didn't even know if He was real.

A CHANGE IN PLANS

In a matter of days, Nadia regained her strength. The bump on her head was still tender, but she knew it was time for her to move on. Her timeline adjusted, however, after meeting a 25-year-old named Jean at a coffee shop. Charming and handsome, he looked like the lead singer of a boy band. Nadia was immediately drawn to him and, when he invited her to dinner, she decided to delay her departure.

Jean showered Nadia with small gifts and a string of compliments. He was everything she ever wanted in a boyfriend.

But her hopes for a lasting relationship were dashed when she discovered he lived in Eastern Europe. He had only flown to her country to conduct a business transaction.

On his final night, before returning home, Jean invited Nadia to join him for a walk.

Holding her hand, Jean said, "Nadia, I know you are young, and we haven't known each other very long ... but I want you to know that I love you. And I have a question to ask: Someday ... would you consider moving to my country and being my wife?"

Nadia stopped and stared into his eyes. "Are you

serious?" she asked.

"Yes," Jean exclaimed. "Very serious."

Nadia answered him with a passionate kiss. "Yes," she said. "I will be your wife."

"You have made me very happy," he said. "Would you consider moving to my country now?"

Nadia hesitated. Leaving her country had never crossed her mind. "I would," she finally said, "but I have no passport or any of the necessary paperwork," she stammered.

"No worries; I can take care of that," he said. "One of my business associates will pick you up next Friday and take you to the airport. That way, I can go home tomorrow and make preparations for the wedding and your arrival."

Again they kissed ... as if sealing their commitment to live together forever.

Friday came and, with deep words of gratitude, Nadia bid farewell to her hosts. They had nursed her back to health and shown her kindness, asking nothing in return. She knew their generosity had something to do with Jesus, but much of it was still a mystery.

Jean's business associate, Leo, escorted Nadia to the airport. "I've been given instructions by Jean to fly with you and make sure you are delivered safely," Leo said in broken English.

"Thank you," Nadia said.

Seated together on the airplane, Leo handed Nadia a piece of paper containing a phone number. "If we get separated, call this number and we will make arrangements. Do you understand?" he asked.

"Yes."

"Good. Jean will be waiting for us."

That thought alone produced a smile on Nadia's face.

Nadia approached the passport control window and surrendered her documents.

"How old are you?" the officer asked.

"Sixteen."

"Are you traveling alone?"

"No, I am traveling with my friend, Leo," she said.

"Where is he?" the officer inquired.

"He's right ..." Nadia cut her answer short. Leo had vanished. "I'm not sure where he went."

"Follow me," the officer ordered.

"What is the problem?" Nadia asked.

"There's a problem with your papers," he announced. "You must come with me."

After several hours of interrogation, Nadia learned she was being transferred to a detention center. Without a proper passport, they said, she would likely be extradited within 72 hours.

"I have come here to be married," she argued, handing them the phone number. "Call this number—Jean or Leo will come for me."

The police officer snatched the paper from her hand ... and Nadia was escorted to an unmarked police car.

RELEASED

Throughout the night, panic and uncertainty ruled Nadia's thoughts. She vowed to keep her eyes open until morning for fear of the hardened women sharing her cell. But, sometime before dawn, she drifted off to sleep. She awoke to the creaking of her metal door.

"Nadia," the officer announced. "There's someone here to see you."

Without hesitation, she darted out the door—hoping and expecting to see Jean. But she was disappointed to see Leo.

"Where did you go?" she asked firmly.

"I'm sorry. It was an accident. We got separated and I couldn't find you. But I'm here now. We straightened everything out."

"Where's Jean?"

"He's meeting us," he said. "He can't wait to see you. I'm taking you to him now."

Nadia followed Leo outside, though beginning to question his story. Seated in the back of his car was a blond-haired man wearing a baseball cap and tinted glasses.

"This is Dirk," Leo said.

Nadia nodded from the front seat.

"Where are we going?" she asked.

Leo sighed hard. "Back to the airport," he said.

"Why?" she clamored.

"I had to tell the police you were in transit ... to another destination ... or they weren't going to release you. Your passport was no good—it cost a lot of money to get you out."

"What about Jean?" she asked.

"He'll be waiting for you when you land."

"Where am I going?"

"Jean wants it to be a secret—you'll find out when you get there."

"Are you flying with me?"

"No," Leo said. "This time you're on your own. Here's your new passport."

The veins in Nadia's neck felt like they could explode. She didn't understand what was happening—she just knew she was in trouble.

When Nadia exited the terminal, she hoped Jean would be waiting to plant a kiss and offer apologies. Instead she heard a chunky man calling her name.

"Nadia? Nadia?" he called. "Are you Nadia?"

"Yes," she said.

"Jean sent me," he said. "Come this way—my car is waiting. I'm supposed to take you to the apartment he has furnished for you."

Reluctantly, Nadia climbed into the car.

Sensing her trepidation, the driver said, "Everything's fine—we're only 20 minutes away."

Nadia sat quietly, soaking in the tall, gray buildings and bridges that dotted the city. Finally the driver broke the ice.

"How old are you?" he asked.

"Sixteen."

"Young."

"Old enough to get married."

"Yes, I heard. Congratulations," he said.

Noting his muted enthusiasm and loss for words, Nadia retreated to her own thoughts.

THE APARTMENT

Although located in a dingy part of town, Nadia was pleased with the furnishings in the apartment. "Much nicer than I thought it would be," she whispered to herself. "But I'll feel a lot better when I see Jean."

More than an hour passed—and Nadia's concerns grew by the minute.

Finally the door opened ... and so did the truth.

Two men—as tall as monsters—flanked a stumpy woman with hoop earrings and penciled eyebrows.

"Welcome, my dear," she said.

"Who are you?"

"I'm your facilitator," she said.

"Facilitator—what's that? Where's Jean?"

"Child, I'm afraid it's time to grow up."

Nadia read between the lines: Jean wasn't coming. Instantly tears streaked Nadia's face.

"If you don't want my two friends here to hurt you, you'll do what I say," the woman said. "Do you understand me?" she growled.

Unable to speak, Nadia nodded.

"You will smile at the men when they arrive and you will make them think you enjoy having sex with them. Because we want them to come back, don't we?" she said sarcastically.

Nadia could have passed for a mannequin.

"One more thing," the woman said. "Your first customer is tomorrow at noon. Don't disappoint me."

To survive—as she had since she ran away at 14—Nadia had learned to conform to any situation. Still, every time she was prostituted, she couldn't help but fight pangs of hatred for Jean and Leo. They had deceived her into a life of abuse.

Several years passed before Nadia had earned enough money and trust that the madam began to take her around town. The madam assumed they were friends. In reality, Nadia despised her.

How can the madam justify what she's done? Nadia

reasoned. *How many lives has she destroyed?*

While shopping together one afternoon, a police officer approached the two women, asking to see their papers. The madam quickly produced hers, but Nadia's were nowhere to be found.

"You can go," the police officer said to the madam, "but I'm afraid you must come with me."

Nadia and the madam exchanged worried glances.

"Where are you taking her?" the madam asked.

"She'll be at the police station until we can verify that she has proper papers."

"Nadia, we will bring your papers," the madam said. "Wait."

Nadia could hear the panic in Madam's voice. Her fear was justified. Under interrogation, Nadia implicated the madam, Jean, Leo and others. In return, the police vowed to relocate Nadia to another city. "You will not be safe here," they said. "These gangs will not stop until they find you—unless we take you far from here."

A NEW COUNTRY

Within days, Nadia found herself in a new country, beginning a new life. That is where she met Amber, who invited her to attend a Christian church.

At first, Nadia resisted. But, in time, Amber began to

remind her of the couple who, years earlier, had befriended her after she had been beaten. *They believed in Jesus, too*, she said to herself. *Maybe I need to check it out for myself.*

After attending her first church service, Nadia refused to miss another one. She committed her life to Jesus and soaked in the uplifting music and encouraging sermons. Still, she found it hard to overcome the pain of her past, at times vowing she could "never trust another human being."

In time, however, Nadia let down her guard and confided in Amber. The two women cried and prayed together as Nadia recounted her story. "I believe Jesus can forgive me," Nadia said, "but I'm not sure I can forgive myself. The shame in my heart is sometimes more than I can bear."

Recognizing that Nadia's emotional scars required the help of a professional, Amber introduced her to Larissa, who served as a caregiver for Project Rescue. That was the beginning of a meaningful friendship, as Larissa helped Nadia move beyond hatred and shame to love and forgiveness.

"You've come a long ways, Nadia," Larissa announced one day. "The other women look up to you—you've given them so much hope."

"God has been good to me," Nadia replied.

"You've shown them that no matter what they've gone through, they don't have to run from their problems," Larissa said. "They can run to Jesus."

"Thank you, Miss Larissa," she said. "I thank God for

you and the Project Rescue home."

Larissa peered up as if savoring a mental image. "I'll never forget the day I first met you and you told me your story," she said. "I thank God that He brought us together—you have become one of my closest friends."

Without warning, tears threatened Nadia's smile. But these were not the tears of sentimental memories. Her heart was aching.

"What is wrong?" Larissa asked.

"I have some disturbing news," Nadia said.

"What is it?"

"I have received confirmation that the men who kidnapped me are on my trail," she stammered.

"We will protect you," Larissa promised.

"No, I must run—they must not find me here," she replied. "It will not be good for you if they do."

"Nadia, you don't have to run anymore."

"Sometimes running is all we can do."

"God will protect you."

"I will pray about it tonight and make my decision tomorrow," Nadia said.

"I will pray, too," Larissa said.

The following morning, Larissa raced into Nadia's room to assure her that God would be her Protector. But she was too late. Nadia had fled during the night. Tears welled up in

Larissa's eyes, as she realized she had likely seen her friend for the last time.

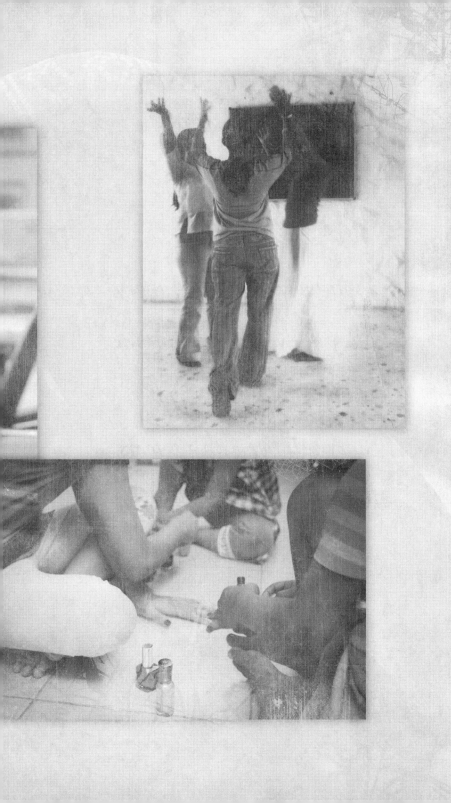

Sumi was tired and hungry,

but finally she had someone

who would listen to her

story. All her pent up tears

threatened to break the banks

of her emotions.

CHAPTER 11

S U M I

Sumi's voice echoed through the clinic's crowded corridor. Though only 9 years old and her voice untrained, she sang with perfect pitch. Had they not seen the lifeless boy in her arms, patients would have assumed she was auditioning for a talent show. Instead, she was just trying to keep her dying brother alive. Malnourished, his eyes were vacant and his legs unable to support his weight.

"Dear little Amshula," she sang with tears sliding down her cheeks. "I know Mommy has died and you're not well, but everything will be okay. You will see—you will be strong again very soon. Everything will be okay."

Sumi's tune was interrupted when a large Scottish woman knifed in front of her and knelt to feel the boy's forehead.

"What's your name?" the woman asked.

"Sumi. This is my brother Amshula. Can you help us?" Sumi asked, her eyes dancing between hope and desperation. "We need ..."

Before she could finish her sentence, the woman took the boy and cradled him in one arm. She pulled back his eyelids to see if he was still conscious.

"Doctor! I need a doctor!" she yelled.

Without a word, a portly nurse ushered them into a room and motioned for the Scottish woman to place him on the bed. With the speed of a battlefield medic, she listened to his heart, administered a shot, and connected him to a bag of intravenous fluids.

"Thank you, nurse," the woman said, patting Sumi's head. "He's going to be okay, right?"

The nurse's face went blank before signaling the foreigner to join her outside.

Breaking her silence, the nurse said, "We know these children. Their mother was a prostitute. She died of AIDS. The boy is HIV positive, too."

"What about their father?"

"He left long ago," the nurse said. "I'm sorry to tell you this, but they are orphans—no one wants them."

"What if I do?" the woman said, almost wishing she could reel back her words.

The nurse paused. "Follow me."

Guiding the woman into an office stacked high with papers, she said, "Our director will join you shortly ... and answer your questions. I will go back and check on the children."

"Thank you," the Scottish woman said.

Moments later, through the flimsy door, she heard the nurse briefing the director.

Finally the tall and slender administrator entered, maneuvering around to his chair.

"Hello, I'm Mr. Jones ... and your name?"

"Miss Tami."

"Are you wanting to adopt the children?" he asked.

"No, I just want to make sure they're taken care of."

"Are you able to pay their medical expenses?"

"I will pay—but I have friends at Project Rescue who will take them in," she said.

"That organization does very good work. Are you sure they will agree?" he asked.

The woman smiled confidently. "Yes," she said.

"They're street kids. We don't have the facilities to keep them here," he noted. "I will tell the authorities I permitted you to take them to Project Rescue, but they are now your responsibility. And you mustn't try to leave the country."

"Is there any paperwork I must sign?"

"A receipt for their medical stay—that's the only documentation you'll need," he replied with a sigh. "We will call you when the boy is well enough to travel."

Six days later, Amshula was sitting upright and eating on his own when Miss Tami collected the two children from the clinic.

Nestling into the backseat of Miss Tami's Land Rover, Sumi threw her arm over Amshula's frail shoulder. "This is the woman that helped us," Sumi said.

Still too weak to speak, Amshula blinked and nodded his appreciation.

"You're safe now," the woman promised. "We're going to take good care of you."

When the Land Rover rolled up to the ministry home, Sumi pressed her face against the window to get a clearer view. Children came running from every direction. The doors swung open and a young woman with an endless smile opened her arms to greet them as the two children climbed out.

"Hi, I'm Lana—and welcome to your new home," the young woman announced.

Sumi glanced at the Scottish woman, then, as if protecting him, roped her arm around Amshula's chest. She pulled him close like a teddy bear to keep him upright.

Lana could see the boy's eyes were fluttering and his lips quivering. She concluded that introductions would have to wait—it was more important to help Amshula to his bed.

BEDSIDE CHAT

Sumi didn't want to leave her brother's bedside that afternoon. They had not been separated since their mother died.

"He'll be okay, Sumi," Miss Tami said. "Go get your bath and eat the meal they've prepared for you. I won't leave until you get back."

"Why must you leave?" the girl asked.

"I don't live here, child. Tomorrow I return to my home in Scotland," she said.

"I thought we were coming to live with you," Sumi said.

"You will be taken care of here. You'll attend school and receive all the help you need. But, after dinner, I want to learn more about you and your brother," she said, abruptly changing the subject.

"Why?" Sumi asked.

"Because I want to think of you—and pray for you—every day we're apart."

"Then I want to tell you now," Sumi said.

Surprised by the child's eagerness, Tami pulled up a chair.

Sumi was tired and hungry, but she finally had someone who would listen to her story. All her pent up tears now threatened to break the banks of her emotions.

"One night Amshula and me came back from looking for food in the garbage field," Sumi began. "We found Mama on the road bleeding. The men she worked for beat her and kicked her out because she was sick."

"Where did you live after that?" Miss Tami asked.

"We lived under some stairs until the owner found us

and made us leave. After that we slept on cardboard in the alley until ..."

Tears surfaced in Sumi's eyes.

"It's okay," Miss Tami said, "if it's too hard to talk about. I understand."

But Sumi marched on. "We took Mama to the hospital, but it wasn't long before she died."

"So, you and Amshula lived alone in the streets after that?"

"Yes—until he got sick, too."

"And is that when you brought him to the hospital?" the woman asked.

"Yes—the day we were lucky to meet you."

"It was more than luck, Sumi," she said. "God sent me to find you."

"To find me?"

"That's right."

"Why would He send you to find me?"

Miss Tami smiled. "I think He wanted you and Amshula to have a home. He wanted you to be safe, to learn how to read and write, and to be in a place where you would have plenty to eat."

Questions swirled in Sumi's head. "Did He tell you where to find us?"

"Not exactly," Tami offered. "I had no reason to be at the clinic that day, but I knew God had led me there for a reason. But when I saw your face, I knew exactly why I was there. God wanted me to help you. He wanted me to bring you to Project Rescue. These are kind people. They will teach you about the God who loved you so much that He gave you a home."

"Will I ever see you again?" Sumi asked.

"I hope so."

Miss Tami leaned over and gave Sumi one last hug. "Go get something to eat ... and I'll stay here and pray for your brother."

Reluctantly Sumi bounced off Miss Tami's lap. She turned and peered into the woman's eyes, again wondering if she'd ever see her again.

Miss Tami smiled and gently squeezed Sumi's hand.

The tiny girl grinned with gratitude. She couldn't get over how Miss Tami's God had sent someone all the way from Scotland just so Sumi and her brother could be rescued and have a home.

Giti collapsed into

Danielle's arms and cried

uncontrollably. She never

wanted to leave the home—

she was just scared that her

life was ending prematurely.

CHAPTER 12

G I T I

With the nimble fingers of an artist, Giti knotted the last wire of the bracelet. She stepped back to admire her handiwork, ensuring that the colorful gemstones were perfectly placed.

"It's beautiful," Danielle, a Project Rescue staff member, said.

"Thank you," Giti said. "I made a matching necklace."

"Very nice," Danielle added with a pat on the shoulder. "Someone will pay you a lot of money for this jewelry."

Giti was pleased that her leader liked the bracelet, because the matching necklace and bracelet were surprise presents for Danielle's 35th birthday.

Danielle had given Giti and the other women more than job skills; she had inspired them to believe that, with God's help, they could overcome their past and lead a productive life. Day after day, she quoted Scriptures of encouragement and lauded their progress.

As Giti surveyed the room filled with women, she

noted one redemptive story after another: Lola was born into a brothel; Svetta was a teenage sex-slave; and Zarina was forced into prostitution as a child. But now they were learning to use sewing machines, operate computers, create jewelry, and more. *They are trophies of God's grace—living proof that He heals and restores*, Giti said to herself. *Danielle has given us so much. I hope I live long enough to do something special for her.*

Tears welled up in Giti's eyes as she reflected on yesterday's shocking news that she was HIV positive. Abruptly she stood from her workstation and retreated to her room. She needed time to pray and cry alone. But bitterness rose inside her like spittle as she pondered her uncle and the disease he had cursed her with.

When Giti was 12, her father died and she was forced to live with an abusive uncle. Day after day, he showered her with insults and obscenities.

"You are worthless," he shouted. "You mean nothing to me."

When she became pregnant with his child, Giti feared he would take her life to dispose of the evidence. All she knew to do was run ... and hope that fate would be kind to her and her baby.

After three days as a fugitive, Giti hobbled into a homeless shelter, clutching her stomach and crying, "I need help." An elderly woman dropped her broom and rushed to the girl's side.

HOMELESS SHELTER

For two months, Giti shared a room with dozens of homeless women and children. She knew she couldn't stay there forever, but where else could she sleep in a warm bed and eat two meals a day?

Each morning, Giti looked forward to a visit from Maurina, the elderly woman who had taken her in. She enjoyed the woman's homemade bread and homespun stories. Maurina was the grandmother Giti never knew.

"Giti," Maurina said one day, "you know this is a temporary shelter. The directors have said you can stay one more week."

"I have nowhere to go," Giti replied.

"I have found you a place," Maurina announced. "It is a home sponsored by Project Rescue. They will help you and your baby."

"These are Christian people," Maurina said. "You can trust them."

"I will miss you, Maurina. I will never forget all you've done for me."

"I will miss you, too," she said. "Someday I hope I have a chance to hold your baby."

"Yes, I hope so, too."

"Can I give you some advice?" Maurina asked.

"Sure."

"I know you've suffered a great deal—and you feel abandoned," she said. "But you're not alone. Jesus loves you and He has a good plan for your life. Listen carefully to what they tell you at Project Rescue. It will give you hope and direction."

"I promise," Giti said, though her mind was teeming with a myriad of questions.

Giti's new home was everything Maurina said it would be. Immediately she felt the love and devotion of Project Rescue's staff. They nursed her through her pregnancy and—when the baby was born—they celebrated together like family members. It didn't take long for Giti to decide she wanted to experience the love, peace and purpose that only Jesus could give. She prayed to receive Jesus as her personal Savior. Her life was almost perfect until HIV reared its ugly head.

THE DISEASE

Danielle saw Giti leave her workstation that day and followed her friend to her room. Giti was facedown on her bed crying when Danielle arrived.

"Giti, what's wrong?" Danielle asked, setting her hand on her back.

Giti rolled over but the tears were still flowing.

"Yesterday I learned I have HIV."

Danielle couldn't shield her grief as tears came to her eyes and she reached to embrace her friend.

"Giti, what about the baby?"

Rubbing her eyes, Giti said, "The baby is fine—no sign of the disease."

"We must tell the other girls so they can pray," Danielle said.

"I will leave the home," Giti told Danielle. "From here on, I can only bring you and the other women misery."

"No—now, more than ever, you belong here," Danielle replied. "We are family."

"I know that," Giti said. "But it's best for me to leave. I just have one question for you: will you take care of my baby when I'm gone?"

"I would do anything for you, but you're not leaving," Danielle said.

"It's not safe," Giti insisted.

"We will take precautions," Danielle countered. "God brought you here—and you're not leaving until He says so." Giti collapsed into Danielle's arms and cried uncontrollably. She never wanted to leave the home—she was just scared that her life was ending prematurely.

"Miss Danielle ..."

"Yes, Giti?"

"If something happens to me, will you make sure my

son follows Jesus?" she asked.

Danielle's tears returned. "You are his mother and you will be here to show him the way."

"Will you promise?" Giti persisted.

"Yes, I'll make sure he learns about Jesus."

With growing enthusiasm, Giti said, "Miss Danielle, I have something for you. It was going to be a birthday present—but I would like to give it to you now."

Danielle smiled, saying, "What is it?"

Giti produced a jewelry box.

"I've never had a necklace this beautiful," Danielle said admiringly. "Thank you so much."

"Remember me every time you wear it," Giti asked.

"I will—but you have many more years ahead of you."

Again the two embraced.

Giti wasn't about to argue with her mentor—but she sensed her days were numbered. Nevertheless, she found comfort in knowing her son was in good hands and, someday, she'd spend eternity with him in heaven.

Ashanti knew her parents loved her. She just resented their unwillingness to stand up to Uncle. His attacks were becoming more frequent and, with each passing day, she felt increasingly helpless and alone.

CHAPTER 13

A S H A N T I

Thirteen-year-old Ashanti leaned against her hovel with her sickly little brother straddling her hip. She could feel Monte's ribs poking through his shirt and hear the strain in his cough. His arms and legs were like twigs, his eyes listless and empty.

Ashanti and Monte waited patiently for their parents to arrive home from a long day behind their kiosk in the downtown market.

But their parents were late—and Monte was fighting to keep his eyes open.

"Little brother," Ashanti said, "I think it's time for you to go to sleep." Sweeping him into her arms, Ashanti returned Monte to his floor mat. She stared at him as he slept, wondering if he would ever recover.

Moments later, the hovel door ripped open. Instantly Ashanti knew it was someone other than her father and mother.

"Ashanti," her uncle called, his voice slurred with alcohol.

Standing before her was a massive man with a soiled

T-shirt covering his potbelly. Gray, greasy whiskers sprouted from his neck and cheeks.

"What do you want?" she asked, trying not to wake Monte.

"I have come to see you," he replied, his eyes full of lust and rage.

"Mama and Papa will be here soon," she warned.

"This won't take long," he said. "Come with me to the bedroom."

Ashanti had nowhere to run. Her uncle grabbed her arm and dragged her onto her parents' bed.

Ashanti's tears were still flowing and Monte was still asleep when their parents arrived home.

"What's wrong?" Mama asked.

"Uncle hurt me again," Ashanti whispered.

"It will be all right," Mama said. "Your uncle is the eldest in the family—he's entitled."

"I don't care—he hurt me," she cried.

"You must not make a scene," Mama said. Disinterested, Papa slipped outside to light a cigarette and Mama grabbed a steel pot to cook dinner.

Ashanti, meanwhile, retreated to her floor mat and cried alone.

Months passed and Monte was playing and laughing again. But even he couldn't protect Ashanti from their uncle's sexual assaults. Instead Monte crawled onto his mat, closed his eyes, and plugged his ears until the nightmares were over. *Someday, when I am bigger, I will stop him*, Monte told himself.

The two children had never attended school. The money their parents earned from the kiosk was just enough to pay their rent and feed the family. School fees were out of the question. But when a "free" after-school tutoring program, sponsored by Project Rescue, opened in the community, Mama made sure her children could attend. To go along with the tutoring, the school promised to provide a new pair of shoes and a warm meal each day.

Many of the children in the tutoring program had never attended school, so Ashanti and Monte didn't feel out of place.

"I love going to school," Ashanti said.

"Me, too," Monte replied.

"I wish I could live at the school all the time," Ashanti added. "That way Uncle wouldn't hurt me anymore."

Ashanti knew her parents loved her. She just resented their unwillingness to stand up to Uncle. His attacks were becoming more frequent and, with each passing day, she felt increasingly helpless and alone.

SECRETS REVEALED

One day, when the tutoring session had ended and it was time to go home, Ashanti tugged on the blouse of Mrs.

Latika. "Can we stay longer?" she asked the Project Rescue caregiver.

"It's late. I think your family will be expecting you," Latika replied.

"My uncle is waiting for me ... and I hate him," Ashanti blurted.

"Why do you hate your uncle?"

"Because he puts his hand over my mouth and touches me—he hurts me."

"Do your parents know what he is doing to you?" Latika asked carefully.

Ashanti could only nod as tears fell down her cheeks.

Latika pulled the child to her chest and held her tight. "What have they told you to do?"

"There's nothing they can do," she whimpered.

Ashanti pulled away from Latika's tear-stained blouse and pled for help with only her eyes.

Well, there's something I can do, Latika said to herself.

Heavy monsoon rains sent market vendors home early one afternoon. Ashanti's parents folded up their kiosk, and headed to Project Rescue to collect their children.

Latika greeted the parents at the door and asked if she could chat with them privately. *God, help me to be strong and determined,* she prayed silently.

"It has come to my attention that Ashanti's uncle has

been abusing her," Latika said.

Ashanti's father grinned. "Our daughter has an active imagination."

"Her uncle has a problem with alcohol, but what she says is not true," her mother added.

"I understand that you feel you must protect him, but this cannot be allowed to continue," Latika said firmly. "If it does, I will report him to the authorities."

"You have no right," her father snapped.

"I have a duty under the law ... and a duty to your daughter."

The father stood to his feet to test Latika's determination. Ashanti's mother remained seated, fighting hard to hide the shame that threatened to monopolize her face.

"Our children will not return to this place," he shouted.

"They will," Latika said, "or you and Ashanti's uncle will be visited by the police."

Ashanti's father clenched his teeth. "We will fight you."

"Then you will lose," Latika said.

The air in the room was thick like steam. "But there is another way," Latika offered. "Let us work with you to protect your children."

"How can you help?" Mama asked.

"When you are at work and not at home, let your children stay here at Project Rescue," she replied.

The parents looked at one another as if cautiously

considering Latika's proposal. Finally they nodded their approval.

"We are not admitting that what you say is true, but the school has been good for our children," Papa said in a much calmer voice.

"We will let them stay," Mama announced.

"Thank you—you won't be sorry," Latika said, grinning widely. "We promise to take good care of Ashanti and Monte."

Hurriedly the parents departed—without a respectful bow or even a shake of Latika's hand. But Latika wasn't complaining. She was just glad they hadn't noticed the beads of perspiration on her forehead or seen the trembling of her hands.

They were already gone when Latika threw her fist in the air and shouted, "Thank You, Jesus."

For two hours the car

zigzagged until it came to

a halt. The two men in the

backseat dragged her up a

flight of stairs before ripping

the duct tape and blindfold

from her face.

CHAPTER 14

S A R A S A

The wedding was a simple one. No bridesmaids or
groomsmen—just a few stand-ins and a minister no one knew.
Sarasa, the bride, wore a plain knee-length dress and the groom,
Juan, donned a pair of slacks and a white dress shirt. The
15-minute ceremony culminated with a customary kiss. But
there was no celebratory recessional for the couple. No music,
rice or laughter. Just the long walk to their modest home.

"I love you," Juan said along the way.

In return, Sarasa could only smile. Although she knew
his words were heartfelt, it would be a long time before she
could reciprocate such words of affection. She could not forget
the ugly circumstances that had brought them together.

The next morning, after Juan left for work, Sarasa
dashed to the telephone. "Mother, I got married yesterday—so
in a few months you can send the children to me," she said, her
voice breaking with joy. "We will send you airplane tickets. The
children will be safe here."

Fortunately, her mother was unaware of the horrible

misfortune that had befallen Sarasa two years earlier when she accepted a job in a distant country. Sarasa promised herself never to tell anyone—including her mother and children—of her nightmare. Because, had her mother known the story, she never would have reunited Sarasa with the children.

Two years earlier, a cousin offered Sarasa a plane ticket and a high paying job in a restaurant. "You will make enough money in six months that you can move your family to a nice home and enroll your kids in a decent school," Enrique promised.

Enrique met Sarasa when her plane landed. He welcomed her with opened arms and a peck on the cheek.

"I am so glad you have come," he said. "To celebrate, I am taking you to dinner and then I'll show you where you'll be staying."

Sarasa nodded as she stared at photographs of her two children.

"Are the children well?" Enrique asked, the car navigating urban traffic.

"Yes," she said. "I will miss them."

"Just remember you are doing this for them," he said.

Sarasa smiled half-heartedly. She had never been separated from her children before.

Enrique knifed into a parking stall outside a restaurant ... just long enough for two men to jump in the backseat. Then he sped away.

"What are we doing?" Sarasa asked, trying not to sound alarmed. "And who are these men, Enrique?"

Enrique shot her a fierce look. "If you make any disturbance, we will kill you and your children," he said. "Believe me when I tell you ... my friends and I will not hesitate to slice your neck. Now give me your passport!"

Sarasa surrendered her documents—her eyes full of terror. One of the men in the backseat blindfolded her and put duct tape on her mouth. For two hours the car zigzagged until it finally came to a halt. The two men in the backseat dragged her up a flight of stairs before ripping the duct tape and blindfold from her face.

"Why are you doing this?" she pleaded.

"Shut up," Enrique screamed, slapping her face. "I promised you a job, didn't I? This is the job!"

"What job?"

"You will pleasure the men I bring you."

"No, I will not go along with this," she said, tears streaming down her face. "I'm your cousin ..."

"Shut up!" he repeated.

"I will not do what you are asking."

"I think she needs some persuasion," one of the men suggested.

Enrique nodded.

Throwing her onto the bed, the men attacked her. At first she struggled and screamed, but she was no match for their brute strength.

After tying her wrists to a bedpost, the two men laughed all the way out the door.

PRISONER

For six months, she never left the apartment. Men cycled through each day as if it were a buffet line, leaving Sarasa on the verge of an emotional breakdown. *If not for my children,* she told herself, *I would have no reason to live.*

One night, Juan walked into the apartment. Like the other men, he had paid to have sex with Sarasa. But, unlike the others, he treated her with the respect of a weekend date—not a victim. He asked her questions about her family and probed her dreams for the future.

"I have no future," she told him one night. "I'll die here."

"I won't let that happen," Juan said. "I've been talking to the owners of this place and have asked if I could buy your freedom, so you can come and live with me."

"I will not be free until I'm reunited with my children," Sarasa said defiantly.

"After we are married, we will send for them," Juan promised.

Sarasa sat up in bed. "Will you do that?"

Juan smiled and fell beside her. "We will be the family

I've always wanted."

FRESH START

Although married to a man she didn't love, Sarasa was filled with anticipation for the day her children would leap into her arms. Juan had rescued her from ruthless criminals and had given her a home. He had begun work on their house in preparation for her kids, and had promised to remain true to his vows. That was enough to earn Sarasa's gratitude and devotion—but she couldn't forget he was once her "customer."

Most days Sarasa walked around a park area, occasionally landing at a bench and letting her tears of regret flow.

One afternoon, a woman noticed her crying and plopped down beside her. "Can I help you?" she asked.

"No, I'm fine," Sarasa said, excusing herself.

But, as fate would have it, they would meet again and again ... in the same place. In time, as they became friends, Sarasa confided her story.

"I know some people who can help you deal with your pain," the woman said. "It is called Project Rescue. Here is the phone number."

Sarasa hid the phone number for a week, before finding the courage to place the call. But that one decision was the beginning of Sarasa's journey to hope and healing.

In the weeks that followed, Sarasa committed her life to Jesus and began to receive counseling and attend a Bible study at Project Rescue. She began to see how Jesus could make everything new. As her faith grew, her bouts with depression waned and, surprisingly, her feelings for Juan soared.

"Sarasa, there's something different about you," Juan said, as they assembled a new bed in anticipation for the children's arrival.

Uncertain how Juan would respond, Sarasa had not divulged her newfound faith. She feared he would be angry and break his promise to reunite her with her children.

"I am feeling healthier," she said flatly.

"No, it's more than that," Juan replied. "There is a glow about you. You seem happier."

"I am happy," she noted. "My children are coming."

"Sarasa, something else has happened—I see it in your eyes," he pressed.

She knew the charade was over. "Something has happened—I have decided to follow Jesus."

Juan paused. "What does following Jesus mean?"

"I'm still learning, but Jesus has brought me a peace," Sarasa said.

"I learned about Jesus when I was a boy," Juan offered, "but I have not prayed to Him in a long time."

"Believe me, Juan—He is real. Since I asked Him

into my life, I've found it easier to forgive. And I'm living for today—not in the past."

Juan swallowed hard. "I have seen what He has done for you. You have changed. I think I would like to know Him, too."

Sarasa pressed close and caressed Juan's hands. Their eyes met in a way they never had before. Sarasa felt something new. "Jesus loves you, Juan," she whispered, "and so do I."

Juan peered into her eyes and saw that her love was genuine. He held her in his arms and kissed her forehead. Finally he had the wife and family he always wanted.

Sarasa basked in Juan's arms for the longest time. She felt his love and devotion ... and knew she was where she belonged. God had brought Juan and Sarasa together for a purpose. And now, because of His mercy and Project Rescue, they would be husband and wife and raise their children to follow Jesus.

APPENDIX I

PROJECT RESCUE AT A GLANCE—1997 TO 2013

- 15 affiliated ministry sites in 6 countries: India, Nepal, Moldova, Tajikistan, Bangladesh and Spain
- 16 aftercare homes for restoration of women/girls who have been in sexual slavery, or for their daughters/sons for prevention
- 4 night-care shelters for children of women in sexual slavery
- 1 aftercare home for restoration of sons of women in sexual slavery
- 6 vocational training centers
- 10 red-light district outreaches
- 2 red-light district churches
- 2 HIV/AIDS clinics
- 6 medical outreaches
- 6 awareness and prevention programs
- Approximately 24,450 women and children ministered to
- Project leader in development of *Hands That Heal: International Curriculum to Train Caregivers of Trafficking Survivors*, launched September 2007 on behalf of FAAST (Faith Alliance Against Slavery and Trafficking)

Projected ministry sites in the next 5 years:

- Russia
- Ukraine
- Turkey

MISSION STATEMENT

We exist to rescue and restore victims of sexual slavery through the love and power of Jesus Christ.

We believe that each child has been created by God with God-given purpose and the innate abilities to accomplish that purpose. We exist to help them discover that purpose and empower them to fulfill it.

We recognize the primary role of the local, national and global community of faith in the restoration process and are committed to empowering them to fulfill it.

We provide global awareness and opportunities for concerned partners to help bring freedom and a transformed future to those imprisoned in sexual slavery.

CORE VALUES

We believe transformational ministries to sexually exploited persons and those at high risk are:

Christ-centered, on the Person and life-changing Truth of Jesus Christ. All hope for genuine new life and freedom is in Him.

Spirit-empowered, recognizing that the battle for freedom from bondage is an epic one between the spiritual forces of darkness and light. This battle for the very lives and souls of exploited women and children must be fought foundationally, locally and individually through the power of the Holy Spirit.

Church-based, growing out of and being supported by the local community of faith. The church is the primary source of faith, intercession, volunteer workers, staff, financial resources, accountability, and sustainability. Ultimately, the church is the support community for the survivors on the healing journey.

Holistic, addressing the multifaceted needs of the whole person as Christ's ministry did—body, mind, and spirit. Without addressing the bondage of slavery on each of these dimensions beyond physical, the victim is not free to choose and live a new life.

Collaborative, seeking to identify other local organizations who are already engaged in some aspect of the multifaceted mission, collaborating in relationship and/or partnership wherever possible for the priority of helping victims of exploitation find new life and healing through Jesus Christ.

VALUE STATEMENT

The Project Rescue team upholds a framework of values to guide the daily actions of our leadership, staff and representatives. These values represent the standards that are used to measure our individual and collective actions.

A commitment to Christ-like character.

Project Rescue is committed to touching the exploited with the love of Jesus Christ. We endeavor to demonstrate His love in practical ways, providing food, a safe home, clothing, education, counseling, vocational training and medical care to rescued victims. We proclaim and endeavor to live God's unconditional love, His provision of forgiveness, and His pathway of acceptance open to all who are broken by sin.

A commitment to treating each person with respect and dignity.

Project Rescue values each individual as a person of eternal value with strengths, weakness, intelligence, emotions and dreams. We help them face the painful traumas of their past to find healing in a loving, supporting community of staff who are committed to their total restoration. The restorative process empowers survivors to face their future with health and hope in Jesus Christ.

A commitment to our partners and employees.

Project Rescue strives to work collaboratively to achieve our goals. We are committed to a ministry environment characterized by continuous learning, passionate faith, and a team orientation. We seek to work with the best-qualified people in the process of restoring victims in order to conduct our mission with professionalism and integrity. All resources entrusted to us are valued as a gift from God to be used effectively, responsibly and accountably in bringing new life to exploited women and girls.

APPENDIX II

PROJECT RESCUE: BEST PRACTICE SUMMARY

1. Recognize that the battle against sexual slavery and for victims' freedom is an epic spiritual battle between good and evil.

2. Effective justice ministry is incarnational and relational, modeled after Christ's incarnate ministry.

3. Learn through assessment before starting any intervention.

4. Understand the complexity of prostituted victims' needs before engaging with them.

5. Collaborate (or network) whenever possible with others sharing the same vision.

6. Start small. "Big" is not always better when entering such an intense ministry with a steep learning curve.

7. Intervention should be local church based, growing out of—and sustained by—the local/national church and community.

8. Money is only a tool to accomplish a God-given mission.

9. Consider the various types of initiatives possible in the local context. What is appropriate and effective in one context may not be effective in another.

10. As a rule, provide aftercare for victims, including children, in family-like settings rather than in institutional homes.

11. Protecting the dignity and privacy of victims must be a constant priority. Compromising either for raising awareness and funds essentially re-exploits victims and survivors.

12. Strive for excellence and professionalism in every aspect of ministry.

13. Choose words for mission, methods and promotion carefully so they give life, add value and reflect Christ.

APPENDIX III

BE PART OF THE SOLUTION

With your help we can provide a safe environment of healing, education and wholeness for those trapped in sexual slavery. Learn how you can be part of creating real and lasting change through the involvements listed below.

PRAY

INTERCEDE FOR:

• **FREEDOM** for every person who is currently a victim of sexual slavery and for survivors that they would be restored spiritually, physically and emotionally.

• **PROVISION** of strong national staff for every ministry site and for their spiritual discernment and authority among staff as they counsel and pray over women, girls and boys in the aftercare homes.

• **RESTORATION** for traffickers and other facilitators of sexual slavery.

ORGANIZE a prayer group using our four-week small group curriculum.

 HOST a prayer walk for victims of sex slavery with our interactive prayer guide.

 SIGN UP for the Project Rescue newsletter to hear about current prayer needs (projectrescue.com).

LEARN

LEARN about sexual slavery at projectrescue.com.

DOWNLOAD the latest Trafficking in Persons report from the U.S. Department of State Office to Monitor and Combat Trafficking.

DOWNLOAD the Nurture Hope Network Tool Kit at www.nurturehope.net under Resources.

SIGN UP for our latest news and information at projectrescue.com.

FIND OUT what is happening in your state. Sign up for the U.S. Policy Alert Service through the Polaris Project at www.polarisproject.com and receive regular updates, maps, and alerts.

RESEARCH trafficking and modern-day slavery by visiting the FAAST (Faith Alliance Against Slavery and Trafficking) website, www.faastinternational.org.

READ

- Grant, Beth and Cindy Lopez Hudlin (2007). *Hands That Heal: International Curriculum to Train Caregivers of Trafficking Survivors.* Springfield, MO: Project Rescue International/ FAAST.

- Grant, David and Beth (2009). *Beyond the Soiled Curtain: Project Rescue's Fight for the Victims of the Sex-slave Industry.* Springfield, MO: Onward Books.

- Bales, Kevin (1999). *Disposable People: New Slavery in the Global Economy.* Los Angeles, CA: University of California Press.

- Barnitz, Laura A. (1998). *Commercial Sexual Exploitation of Children: Youth Involved in Prostitution, Pornography & Sex Trafficking.* Washington, D.C.: Master Print, Inc.

- Batstone, Kevin (2007). *Not for Sale: The Return of the Global Slave Trade—and How We Can Fight It.* New York, NY: HarperCollins.

- Ehrenreich, Barbara and Arlie Russell Hochschild, eds. (2002). *Global Woman: Nannies, Maids and Sex Workers in the New Economy.* New York: Henry Holt & Company.

- Farr, Kathryn (2005). *Sex Trafficking: The Global Market in Women and Children.* New York, NY: Worth Publishers.

- Farley, Melissa, ed. (2004). *Prostitution, Trafficking, and*

Traumatic Stress. Haworth Maltreatment and Trauma Press.

• Haugen, Gary (2009). *Good News About Injustice: Updated 10th Anniversary Edition: A Witness of Courage in a Hurting World*. Downers Grove, IL: InterVarsity Press.

• Jewell, Dawn (2008). *Escaping the Devil's Bedroom: Sex Trafficking, Global Prostitution, and the Gospel's Transforming Power*. Grand Rapids, MI: Monarch Books.

• Kara, Siddharth (2009). *Sex Trafficking: Inside the Business of Modern Slavery*. New York, NY: Columbia University Press.

• Kasten, Liora and Jesse Sage, eds. (2008). *Enslaved: True Stories of Modern Day Slavery*. New York, NY: Palgrave MacMillan.

• Kilbourn, Phyllis and Marjorie McDermid, eds. (1998). *Sexually Exploited Children: Working to Protect and Heal*. Monrovia, CA: MARC.

• Malarek, Victor (2003). *The Natashas: Inside the New Global Sex Trade*. New York, NY: Arcade Publishing.

• Malarek, Victor (2009). *The Johns: Sex for Sale and the Men Who Buy It*. New York, NY: Arcade Publishing.

• McCormick, Patricia (2006). *SOLD*. New York, NY: Hyperion Paperbacks for Children.

• McGill, Craig (2003). *Human Traffic: Sex, Slaves &*

Immigration. London, England, UK: Vision Paperbacks.

- Metzler, Milton (1993). *Slavery: A World History.* New York, NY: Da Capo.

- Miles, Glenn and Josephine-Joy Wright, eds. (2003). *Celebrating Children: Equipping People Working with Children and Young People Living in Difficult Circumstances Around the World.* Carlisle, Cumbria, UK: Paternoster Press.

- Singer, P.W. (2006). *Children at War.* Berkeley, CA: University of California.

- Skinner, Benjamin A. (2009). *A Crime So Monstrous: Face-to-Face with Modern-day Slavery.* New York, NY: Free Press.

WATCH

- *Nefarious: Merchant of Souls* (2012)
- *Blood Diamond* (2006) illustrates how child soldiers are used in West African conflicts.
- *Soldier Child* (2005), a documentary about child soldiers in Uganda
- *Born into Brothels: Calcutta's Red Light Kids* (2005)
- *Fields of Mudan* (2004), a 23-minute film about child sex slavery in Asia
- *Sex + Money: A National Search for Human Worth* (2007)

- *Human Trafficking* (2005), the 4-hour Lifetime miniseries on European women trafficked into the USA for prostitution
- *Amazing Grace* (2007), the inspiring true story of William Wilberforce who demanded abolition of the African slave trade in the UK in the 1800s
- *Modern-Day Slavery: Sierra Leone and Liberia*, a 10-minute video by World Hope and World Relief
- *Sex Trafficking in Cambodia* (2003), a 23-minute World Hope video documenting the lives of victims in Cambodia
- *Trade* (2007); sex trade into the United States
- *Holly* (2007), a 1-hour, 54-min. movie on child trafficking in Cambodia
- *Very Young Girls* (2007), a documentary by G.E.M.S. about domestic human trafficking in New York

EDUCATE

TALK about sex slavery and trafficking with your family, friends, co-workers, and leaders.

HOST a small group using our four-week small group curriculum.

ATTEND a Project Rescue event in your area. Find out about upcoming activities on our events page at projectrescue.com.

FEATURE Project Rescue at your church, school, Bible study, or other community forum.

INTRODUCE a book or movie on sexual slavery into your book club, Sunday school, or other gathering.

WRITE articles and/or letters of opinion for local papers, church, or other publications.

ADVOCATE

ASK your state legislators what they've done to stop trafficking and labor trafficking in your state. If they don't know, offer to provide information on what they can do.

FIND OUT if your state has an Anti-Trafficking Task Force. More information on state action is available at www.polarisproject.com.

TEACH young adults about the link between pornography, trafficking and sexual slavery. Stop demand before it starts.

SERVE

ORGANIZE an anti-trafficking group in your school or church.

ENGAGE with an existing social service agency to help survivors of sex slavery.

APPLY for Project Rescue's six-week summer internship.

REPORT TRAFFICKING

LEARN how to identify victims of sexual slavery and trafficking from the U.S. Department of Health and Human Services Rescue & Restore Campaign.

REPORT any information or potential slavery activity near you to the National Human Trafficking Resource Center Hotline at (888) 373-7888. Your call could save lives.

GIVE

VISIT the Project Rescue donation page at www.projectrescue. com to give now.

MAIL donations to Project Rescue, P.O. Box 922, Springfield, MO 65801.

CONTACT Project Rescue to host a fundraiser at your church or community center.

BUY products made by women in Project Rescue affiliated vocational training centers through the UCount Campaign or The Jubilee Market. Information at www.projectrescue.com.

* Portions of information adapted from the Faith Alliance Against Slavery and Trafficking.

ENDNOTES

STATISTICS

1. Free the Slaves, "Top 10 Facts About Modern Slavery," http://www.freetheslaves.net/Page.aspx?pid=375 (accessed December 8, 2010).

2. UNICEF; quoted in U.S. Department of State, "Trafficking in Persons Report," 10th ed. (Washington, D.C.: U.S. Department of State, 2010), p. 12.

3. International Labor Office, A Global Alliance Against Forced Labor, "Global Report Under the Follow-up to the ILO Declaration on Fundamental Principles and Rights at Work" (Geneva: 2005), p. 55, http://www.ilo.org/global/publications/ ilo-bookstore/order-online/books/WCMS_081882/lang—en/ index.htm (accessed December 9, 2010).

4. Random History, "55 Litle Known Facts About ... **Human Trafficking**," http://facts.randomhistory.com/human-trafficking-facts.html.

5. "Bangladesh (Tier 2)," http://www.state.gov/documents/ organization/192594.pdf, p. 81.

6. "Country Profiles: India," http://asia-pacific.undp.org/practices/hivaids/documents/HIV_and_Mobility_in_South_Asia_web_India.pdf.

7. "Picture in India," http://www.unicef.org/india/children.html.

8. United States Department of Labor, "2011 Findings on the Worst forms of Child Labor – Moldova, 26 September 2012," http://www.unhcr.org/refworld/docid/5065941b27.html (accessed April 6, 2013), p. 1.

9. U.S. Department of State, "Trafficking in Persons Report: June 2012," http://www.state.gov/documents/organization/192597.pdf, p. 320.

INTRODUCTION

1. Yamiche Alcindor, "That's Slavery," *USA Today* (September 27, 2012).

2. United Nations Office on Drugs and Crime, www.unodc.org (2013).

3. U.S. Department of State, Office to Monitor and Combat Trafficking in Persons.

4. Alcindor, op. cit.

5. Johns Hopkins University, www.protectionproject.com (2013).

6. Kevin Bales, *Disposable People: New Slavery in the Global Economy* (Los Angeles: University of California Press, 1999).

7. Lisa Thompson, "Introduction to the Global Issue of Human Trafficking," in Beth Grant and Cindy Lopez Hudlin, *Hands That Heal: International Curriculum to Train Caregivers of Trafficking Survivors* (Springfield, MO: Project Rescue International/FAAST, 2007), p. 27.

8. Phyliss Kilbourn, *Hands That Heal*, p. 17.

ABOUT THE AUTHORS

David and Beth Grant serve as co-founders and directors of Project Rescue. They are compassionate voices mobilizing people of faith to extend hope and healing to those devastated by sexual slavery.

For 40 years, the 1.2 billion people of India have been at the heart of the Grants' efforts, though their passion has carried them to more than 30 countries. While continuing their commitment to the people of India, David and Beth are casting vision for the development of new Project Rescue affiliated ministries across Eurasia and Europe. David is a contagious, passionate communicator who motivates people of faith to engage generously in meeting physical and spiritual needs around the world. Beth is a cross-cultural educator focused on developing initiatives that enable women to discover their God-given identity and purpose—whether they find themselves in a brothel or a boardroom.

David and Beth serve on the steering committee of the Faith Alliance Against Slavery and Trafficking (FAAST), based in Washington, D.C. In partnership with FAAST, Beth co-edited *Hands That Heal, International Curriculum to Train Caregivers of Trafficking Survivors* (2007). David is engaged in a doctoral program in Leadership Development at the Assemblies of God Theological Seminary. Beth earned a Ph.D. in Intercultural Education from Biola University in Los Angeles, California.

David and Beth have two married daughters, Rebecca and Jennifer, who share their parents' heart for ministry to victims of sexual exploitation. Rebecca founded Rescue Arts, which uses creative arts for healing with survivors of sexual exploitation and trafficking (www.rescuearts.com). After serving two years with Chi Alpha Campus Ministries at Colorado State University and representing Project Rescue and Rescue Arts, Rebecca, husband Tyler Shults, and baby Judah are preparing to serve in India with university students and Rescue Arts. Jennifer works as a director of nursing. Her husband, Jonathan Barratt, serves with Project Rescue in business administration and development. He and Jennifer recently welcomed baby Gemma, increasing the Grants' joy in their new role as grandparents.

AN OPPORTUNITY

_____ YES, I want to help rescue young women and children from sexual slavery.

_____ $30 per month will provide night-care shelter for a child whose mother is in the red-light district.

_____ $100 per month will provide care for a rescued victim living in an aftercare home.

_____ $1,200 per month will cover operational expenses for an aftercare home.

_____ $100,000 will help provide an aftercare home.

Name _____

Address _____

City/State/Zip_____

Phone _____

E-Mail Address _____

_____ Please add me to your e-newsletter.

PROJECT RESCUE

P.O. Box 922 / Springfield, MO 65801 / 417-833-5564

www.projectrescue.com

Donations: Project Rescue, AGWM Acct. #6149520 (40)

All contributions are tax-deductible as allowed by law.

TO MAKE A DIFFERENCE

FOR MORE INFORMATION

CONTACT:

Project Rescue

P.O. Box 922

Springfield, MO 65801

417-833-5564

projectrescue@projectrescue.com

www.projectrescue.com

For information on Onward Books:

www.onwardbooks.com

Onward Books, Inc.

4848 S. Landon Ct.

Springfield, MO 65810

417-425-4674